HAWAII AND ITS GODS

Hawaii

and Its Gods

text by
CHARLES F. GALLAGHER

photographs by
DANA LEVY

with a foreword by
O. A. BUSHNELL

WEATHERHILL/KAPA
New York, Tokyo & Honolulu

THE ENDPAPERS: The front endpaper shows an engraving from a drawing by Jacques Arago of officers from the French corvette Uranie visiting a *heiau* on the island of Hawaii during the French exploring expedition of 1819 under Louis de Freycinet. The back endpaper reproduces an engraving, also based on drawings by Arago, of the baptism on board the Uranie of High Chief Kalanimoku, prime minister and treasurer of the Kingdom of Hawaii, in Honolulu Harbor in August 1819. Among the Hawaiian dignitaries in attendance were King Kamehameha II, the Dowager Queen Kaahumanu, and Boki, governor of Oahu. (Engravings reproduced by courtesy of the Archives of Hawaii)

First edition, 1975

Published by John Weatherhill, Inc., 149 Madison Avenue, New York, N.Y. 10016, with editorial offices at 7-6-13 Roppongi, Minato-ku, Tokyo 106, Japan, and Kapa Associates Ltd., 677 Ala Moana Boulevard, Honolulu, Hawaii 96813. Protected by copyright under terms of the International Copyright Union; all rights reserved. Printed and first published in Japan.

Library of Congress Cataloging in Publication Data: Gallagher, Charles F / Hawaii and its gods. / 1. Hawaii—Religion. I. Levy, Dana, ill. II. Title. / BL2620.H3G34 / 200'.9969 / 74-28153 / ISBN 0-8348-2501-5

CONTENTS

FOREWORD

PEOPLE WHO LIVE UPON ISLANDS borrow foods and fashions, ideas and attitudes, genes and religions from people who live in the great world beyond their shores. People who live upon islands are hospitable to imported thoughts as well as to strangers and the gifts they bear. Islanders must be hospitable in their isolation, else they will languish and die, as much from a lack of new thoughts as from a deficiency of such treasures as gasoline and paper towels.

Because the islands of Hawaii are among the most isolated habitable places on earth, the people who have come to live in them have been importing things and ideas ever since the first Polynesians arrived about twelve hundred years ago. Since 1778, when Captain James Cook and his mariners discovered Hawaii for the Western world, the process of borrowing has been accelerated. Things and thoughts, borrowed freely and extravagantly from all parts of the world, brought in by design or by accident, have transformed these islands. Where once they were raw and brutal masses of rock, little more than mountains of lava risen from the sea, they were changed to hanging gardens that became as fair to look upon and to live in as any place yet found on earth. The greatest transformation of all affected the inhabitants themselves. They, too, borrowed people from nations the world around; and most of the children their matings produced are the handsomest improvements upon their ancestors that any hopeful parents could ask for.

As a consequence of these exuberant borrowings, Hawaii's people today—especially those who live in Honolulu—are cultivated, cosmopolitan, ecumenical to a degree that was beyond imagining in 1940 as well as in 1778. They enjoy all the benefits —and suffer many of the horrors—of the modern international culture; and they are acquainted with all the comforts and stimuli for both body and psyche that people in the seven continents and the five seas have discovered. This richness, this prodigality of choices, of course, is one of the reasons why living in Hawaii can be so pleasant—and so expensive.

One of the problems with living in Hawaii today, however, is the simple fact that we are being rather overwhelmed by all these importations. We are all so busy—borrowing still, changing, exchanging, selecting, rejecting, running around to try all these exciting new things that are being devised, whether in New York, Paris, Tokyo, Rio de Janeiro, or Honolulu—that we don't quite know anymore what we can find at home in our islands. And we are reaching the point where we do not know how to enjoy the many gifts that our predecessors have presented to us. Like islanders everywhere, we are still insular. Despite all our advantages, despite our cosmopolitan position at the very crossroads of the Pacific, we are still isolated.

This abiding insularity is exactly the reason why people who live upon islands need to be visited by "outsiders." In Hawaii a kinder word for them is *malihinis*, or newcomers, as we entrenched *kamaainas* call them. *Malihinis* have a way of seeing things that *kamaainas* overlook or take for granted, of asking questions about matters *kamaainas* have forgotten or never think about, of taking superb photographs of places that *kamaainas* have never seen, of writing books and making remarks upon subjects about which *kamaainas* have been serenely unaware.

Charles F. Gallagher and Dana Levy, the colleagues who present us with this handsomely illustrated account, are *malihinis* of the kind that we Hawaiians like best. They are citizens of the world to an extent that may well awe even the most cosmopolitan Hawaiian. Mr. Gallagher, an American Universities Field Staff representative, spends half of each academic year as Consultant on International Relations at the University of Hawaii in Honolulu, the rest of the year in Rome, or Madrid, or Tokyo, or others of the world's great cities as Director of Studies of that consortium of universities. Inasmuch as he has been visiting Hawaii since 1937, he has good reason to resent being called a *malihini*. But because he looks at us and our islands with the detached and appraising intelligence we attribute to outsiders (and too rarely find among our biased selves), we must deny him the status of a *kamaaina*.

Dana Levy, a designer and photographer, was born and educated in California. For the past several years he has lived in Tokyo as art director of John Weatherhill, Inc. He is the artist who has designed many of those supremely beautiful books that are published by Weatherhill. One of the most distinguished of those books, *Bamboo*, a photographic essay about that superlative plant and its many uses, was designed and illustrated by Mr. Levy. His most recent book is *Water: A View from Japan*. At present he is preparing a book on Japanese baths and bathhouses.

Mr. Gallagher and Mr. Levy have turned their outsiders' attention upon an aspect of our life in Hawaii that we ourselves have neglected. In this fine book they are showing us that, in the course of acquiring all the artifacts and concepts developed in the great world, the people of Hawaii also have imported an amazing number of religions. These two *malihinis* are reminding us—with some of the most beautiful photographs ever taken in our islands and with an enlightened complementary text—not only that our churches and temples are interesting borrowed things in their own solid right, but also that the religions which built those edifices are still a living part of our heritage. To us, as to them, the *heiaus* of indigenous Hawaiians cannot be dismissed as mere heaps of stones, relics of a dead and ancient past. Although in all the islands, "from Hawaii in the east to Niihau in the west," as once their poets sang, not a single *heiau* has been restored, the great gods, spirit guardians, and lesser deities who were worshiped there in the days of old dwell in them yet. Some of us can feel their presence still when we enter those sacred precincts.

Most of us will be surprised to discover that so many theologies, denominations, and sects have been established in these islands. We should not be: the people we have borrowed hastened to borrow the comforts they wanted from the countries that loaned their people to us. Many of us will be astonished to see illustrated here the varieties in styles of art and architecture with which our borrowed people have adorned their houses of worship. All of us should rejoice at this diversity: we are in good health when shrines and temples from the Orient, gorgeous with gold and cinnabar, sit in our landscape as naturally as do the austere chapels of New England or the tiny, sad confections built by parishioners in hinterland Hawaii. And certainly a few of us should sorrow for those homesick Catholic priests from civilized France and Belgium who, with house paints, loving labor, and the crafty magic of *trompe l'oeil*, captured visions of Europe's great cathedrals in the narrow boxes of parish churches lost in the desolation of Kona and Ka'u.

For everyone who reads this book, whether as *kamaaina* or as *malihini*, in Hawaii or away from it, the message from its authors is clear. It is another testimony to Hawaii and its aloha.

FOREWORD

They are telling us that these temples and churches, whether they are old or new, beautiful in your eyes or ugly, of Oriental provenance or Occidental, are treasures to be cherished. We must cherish them because they are manifestations of the happy commingling of peoples and faiths that is our finest exportable gift to the world beyond our shores.

O. A. Bushnell

Honolulu

HAWAII AND ITS GODS

The Ancient Way

ANCIENT POLYNESIA WAS ALSO a dark and bloody land. The romantic notion that the islands of the South Pacific were in olden times the home of noble savages has been slow in dying. Distance long lent enchantment to this as to other dreams, and those eighteenth-century Europeans who were looking in vain for a perfect and civilized realm, as in China half a world away, were only too eager to persuade themselves that pagan paradises had also been found in the far stretches of the Pacific by Bougainville, Tasman, and finally Cook. The myth that helped spawn the great South Sea Bubble, which ended in disaster after serious men had lost life savings in the pursuit of the unattainable, was laid low only briefly before it emerged again a hundred years later in the writings and paintings of Melville, Stevenson, Twain, and Gauguin.

The images that the works of these nineteenth-century artists conjured up were inherited by a later wave of the faithful closer to our time: Rupert Brooke, Nordhoff and Hall, Michener, and many others who refined the legend without defining the reality that gave it birth. Still other men laid hands on the pliant vision and shaped it to their own ends: the makers of the tragic and sentimental films of the early decades of this century—Murnau, Flaherty, Van Dyke; the composers of the half-native, half-foreign ballads that program the sight of Polynesia with their unmistakable sound; and the thousands engaged in the trade of bringing the multitudes of the world to these many islands, whose culture and history have been so profoundly refurbished and reworked that the dream became father to the fact; and the legend, however fleetingly, was turned into a form of the evanescent truth that all men pursue under the name of beauty.

The true magic of Hawaii—and of its sister island chains scattered across the Polynesian Pacific—is just this: that it has become for a moment in eternal time what many men over many centuries have wanted it to be. The self-fulfilling wish ended by creating a modern version of paradise for modern men, ultimately to be lost again by them, but one that harked back in its roots to pagan shores on which there was neither bread nor wine, neither metal nor the wheel, neither the written word of man nor the scripture of God, and little hope or charity: a garland of islands, the most isolated of all human societies, knowing no other and having no counterpoint of men different from themselves, lost in the endless space of the open sea and cut off in time from everything but the legendary memory of a dimly distant homeland beyond the western waters—Havaiki, the ancestral abode of their Polynesian forefathers—ignorant of the outside world and in turn unknown by it over the long count of centuries.

* * *

In ancient Hawaii, as in all primitive cultures, society was delicately balanced, in subtle equilibrium with the forces of nature, and the actions of men were carefully regulated for the purpose of keeping order in heaven and on earth. Existence was thought of as a unity embracing all aspects of life, but was expressed in a symbiotic dualism of opposites: light (*ao*) and darkness (*po*); life and death; healing magic and sorcery; and the *kapu* system that separated the prerogatives and duties of the sexes and the social classes—chiefs and commoners.

Often this dualism was implicit but inherent, as in that pertaining to Ku—the god who freed one from his faults and errors, hence his association with the sacrifice of prisoners in later times in his manifestation as Ku-ka-ilimoku, the god of war—and Lono, the bringer of rain and dispenser of fertility, hence the god of the bountiful harvest, Lono-i-ka-makahiki; or between Kane—the creator and giver of life, associated with the sun, the sky, and dawn—and Kanaloa, the old Polynesian sea god, connected with water, darkness, and death.

The ancient Hawaiian belief system produced another kind of duality. On the one hand is found a highly poetic and moving vision of the cosmos, of the concept of man and his infinitesimal place in it, and of the innate harmony of all the living phenomena of the finite and infinite worlds. On the other, there existed a harsh and oppressive social system that evolved as the expression of an involuted and minutely detailed framework of religious proscriptions and obligations that is the obverse of the profundity and refined elegance of the religious tradition at its highest level.

The opening lines of the *Kumulipo*, the famous Hawaiian creation chant, express the first of these concepts—the delicate reverence for universal life—with the utmost poetic imagery as they describe the emergence of life itself from primeval darkness:

O ke au i kahuli wela ka honua
O ke au i kahuli lole ka lani
O ke au i kuka'iaka ka la
E ho'omalamalama i ka malama
O ke au o Makali'i ka po
O ka walewale ho'okumu honua ia
O ke kumu o ka lipo, i lipo ai
O ke kumu o ka po, i po ai
O ka lipolipo, o ka lipolipo
O ka lipo o ka la, o ka lipo o ka po
Po wale ho'i

O paia'a i ke auau ka manawa
O he'e au loloa ka po
O piha, o pihapiha
O piha-u, o piha-a
O piha-e, o piha-o
O ke ko'o honua pa'a ka lani

O lewa ke au, ia Kumulipo ka po
Po no

At the time when the earth became hot
At the time when the heavens turned about
At the time when the sun was darkened
To cause the moon to shine
The time of the rise of the Pleiades
The slime, this was the source of the earth
The source of the darkness that made darkness
The source of the night that made night
The intense darkness, the deep darkness
Darkness of the sun, darkness of the night
Nothing but night
Multiplying in the passing time
The long night slips along
Fruitful, very fruitful
Spreading here, spreading there
Spreading this way, spreading that way
Propping up earth, holding up the sky
The time passes, this night of Kumulipo
Still it is night

There is an intimate link between the poetic vision and the harsh reality. For the great legend cycles of old Hawaii like the *Kumulipo*, handed down orally for countless generations and written down only in the nineteenth century, were more than poetic chants and genealogical recitals, even though they include both these facets. They are cosmological constructions that link the whole Hawaiian race through its chiefs to "the sacred spark in man from its inception to its maturity into a divinity born as a human being on earth to carry on the family ruling line."

It is through this linkage that the sacred power, or mana, of the universe is transmitted to the rulers and chiefs, who guard it jealously and dispense it to their subjects through their very being. The concept of mana as the instrument by which divine authority is transformed into earthly power is essential to understanding how the social system of ancient Hawaii, and in particular the *kapu* or taboo system, came into being and evolved in time.

The primary goal of the noble, or *ali'i*, class was acquiring, maintaining, and if possible enhancing mana for oneself and one's family; and it can be seen that this was a religious as well as a secular objective. It involved an almost constant struggle for power among contending chiefs in a very limited area. For just as mana blurred the lines between the divinity of the gods and the sacredness of the chiefs who inherited from those gods, it also intertwined the idea of an inherited divine right to superiority and the capability of exercising that right effectively. In the real world of primitive survival it was not enough for an *ali'i* to claim the right to rule by virtue of his genealogy; he had to prove his superiority by vanquishing rival chiefs and their supporters in battle and taking their lands. The struggles were bitter and treacherous, and the slaughter or sacrifice of survivors was an essential ingredient of the mana-acquisition system. The gods favored the victors, not those with the best genealogies, and for the vanquished there was no place to hide.

The belief system and the rank system, and the power structure that upheld both, were thus all tied together, and the ensemble was based on two pillars: purification and sacrality, the quality of sacredness. The ritual purity necessary for the individual to make his way through the dangers of life that existed on all sides in countless forms was obtainable by correctly performing ceremonial rites under the direction of priests, or *kahuna*, who alone knew the magic formulas that would provide security and prosperity. The *kahuna* were consulted in every life crisis from birth to death, and for purposes good and evil. They provided remedies for illness, arranged for easy childbirth, made barren women fertile, made prophecies, read omens and interpreted signs, cleansed defiled persons and places, and engaged in magic and sorcery of all kinds. There were numerous classes of *kahuna*, divided according to their skills and their methods of practice. Among the most important in many respects were the chiefs' agents, the *ilamuku*, who were responsible for enforcing the *kapu*.

The *kapu* itself was the second pillar of the system, and the term is best translated as "the quality of sacredness." Although the idea of prohibition is manifest in the term—and it is in this way that it is normally interpreted in Hawaii today—the basic concept is that of an aura of protective sanctity that surrounds or is put around a person, a place, or an object. The *kapu* was also closely connected with the ranking system. Different grades of high chiefs and ruling chiefs had different degrees of *kapu* and were entitled to varying degrees of veneration. Children inherited from both parents and could thus attain an even higher degree of sacredness than was possessed by either progenitor.

The *kapu* of the most noble chiefs was such that their feet could not touch the ground nor their shadow fall on a house for fear that accidental contact would contaminate the object so touched with excessive sacrality and thus make it unusable. Conversely, such a chief was said to have the prerogatives of the prostrating taboo (*kapu moe*), whereby the common people were required to lie flat on the ground in his presence, and the burning taboo (*kapu wela*), by the terms of which violators might be condemned to death by fire. In other cases punishment might take the form of strangling, drowning, or clubbing the offender to death.

The *kapu* of the highest chiefly rank, involving brother-and-sister marriage, which was deemed eminently desirable, was equal to that of the gods themselves. All objects connected with the person of such a high-ranking individual were *kapu*, and contact with such items as his mat, his *tapa* cloths, or his loincloth (*malo*) by any person not consecrated for personal service meant punishment by being burned to death. Indeed, because of the *kapu* of their shadow it was difficult for the highest-ranking chiefs to go about during the day, and they were forced to meet with lower-ranked persons principally after sunset.

Because of the extreme severity of the system, some chiefs deliberately hid their high rank when they went into the countryside, preferring to travel incognito partly so that commoners would not die because of violating their *kapu*, but also partly to escape the ultimately stifling effects of the onerous system.

Besides the chiefly class, there were two other groupings: the commoners (*maka'ainana*) and the outcasts (*kauwa*). The latter were often those designated to serve the chiefs and touch them directly. They were thus exempted from the *kapu* but paid a heavy price in being considered unclean. It was not proper to eat with them or sleep close to them, and in their function as personal slaves they were buried alive upon the death of their masters, and were often offered in sacrificial atonement for *kapu* violations committed by their overlords. The common people, especially those in outlying areas, seldom came in contact with the chiefs and were to a considerable extent spared constant involvement with the intricacies of the *kapu* system, except on those holidays and feasting periods that were sacred to the various gods.

The legal system rested on the foundation of *kapu* but was augmented by edicts (*kanawai*), which might be issued by ruling chiefs at any time, or whose origin in antiquity led to their being considered commands of the gods. Many of these were enlightened and humane decrees, of which a famous example was the Edict of the Splintered Paddle (*kanawai mamalahoa*), laid down by Kamehameha the Great (reigned c. 1795–1819). Allegedly proclaimed by that ruler in gratitude for his having barely escaped death in a raid against a rival war party, it established a code of safe conduct for travelers throughout his realm, which he enforced on a later occasion to the extent of sparing a traveling party of his enemies against the advice of his own supporters—a most uncommon happening at the time.

The sacred edicts of the ruling chiefs were called a "life-giving refuge" (*pu'uhonua ho'ola*). Just as the space immediately surrounding the person of the ruler was a sacred area within which one could escape death or punishment, so by extension were these edicts, and both were complemented by their enlarged territorial counterpart, the *pu'uhonua* places of refuge, designated sacred areas to which men might repair and be safe from reprisal. The *pu'uhonua* areas, of which the only surviving and somewhat atypical one is the City of Refuge at Honaunau on the island of Hawaii, were sacrosanct land within the confines of which no blood could be shed. In later life Kamehameha the Great made all the lands belonging to his favorite consort, Kaahumanu, into *pu'uhonua* territory; and he did the same with those dedicated to the war god, Ku, whose caretaker he had been in his youth and under whose standard he had conquered and unified all the islands of Hawaii by 1810. The faith that Kamehameha had placed in Ku, whose epithet *ka-ilimoku* means "land-grabber," had been amply vindicated by the course of history, and the granting of the refuge areas was the monarch's grateful repayment for the god's help.

The society that evolved over centuries within this tightly knit framework of ritual and rivalry, of prohibition and propitiation, was one dominated by awe and insecurity. There was a widespread and compelling personal fear of the all-powerful gods and the godlike chiefs, of the phenomena of nature, and of the invisible spirit world that surrounded man on all sides. The virtually unceasing struggle of chiefly factions for land, retainers, and power made all dominion uncertain and usually temporary, and kept the chiefs themselves unsure and suspicious.

A native authority writing a century ago suggested that the common people were worse off. They owned no land in their own right—all land was held in the name of the ruler, who bestowed it at his pleasure on the ruling chiefs, who allocated it to their followers, who in turn allowed the commoners to avail themselves of it on sufferance and in return for the payment of crop tribute—nor did they have incentives to produce more and better foodstuffs and products lest these be taken by their masters. They were required to follow their chiefs and die without question in wars of prestige and quarrels of personal status that were alien to their concerns. They had to perform corvée service at their superiors' demand, and they were subject to capricious plunder at all times, even, as the nineteenth-century chronicler noted, during the autumnal *makahiki* festival dedicated to Lono, which was nominally a time for rest and rejoicing:

"Much wealth was acquired by the [*makahiki*] god during this circuit of the island in the form of tribute (*ho'okupu*) from the *moku'aina, kalana, 'okana,* and *ahupua'a* land sections at certain places and at the boundaries of the *ahupua'a*. There the wealth was presented—pigs, dogs, poi, tapa cloth, dress tapas (*'a'ahu*), *'oloa* tapa, *pa'u* skirts, *malo* loincloths, shoulder capes (*'ahu*), mats, *ninikea* tapa, *olona* fishnets, fishlines, feathers of the *mamo* and the *'o'o* birds, finely designed mats (*'ahu pawehe*), pearls, ivory, iron (*meki*), adzes, and whatever other property had been gathered by the *konohiki*, or land agent, of the *ahupua'a*. If the tribute presented by the *konohiki* to the god was too little, the attendant chiefs of the god (*po'e kahu ali'i akua*) would complain, and would not furl up the god nor twist up the emblems and lay him down. The attendants kept the god upright and ordered the *ahupua'a* plundered. Only when the keepers were satisfied with the tribute given did they stop this plundering (*ho'opunipuni*) [in the name] of the god. Most of the wealth received in this circuit of the god was given to the crowd—to the people who attended to the god, to those who carried the image, to the people in the procession."

*   *   *

How then did the commoners bear their burdens? In the largest sense it might be said that the utter isolation of their society in time and space offered to the people no other model and gave them no glimmer that there might be anything different from the lot that had befallen them. Theirs was a land without time, consumed in an endless present, and they themselves were a people whose oral chronicles, their only link with the past, reinforced the sanctions of religion and the authority of their gods and chiefs.

Still, the ancient Hawaiians managed to find an escape from the rigors of a highly ritualized existence in the naturalness of their lives in a benign climate. There was time for games and athletic contests, and for playing in the gentle seas around them. They found comfort in their unthinkingly shared acceptance of fate and in their communal cooperativeness. Life was lived at a simple level that united the soft fertility of the land with the easy sexuality of man. Existence was literally existential, and begetting, becoming, and dying were part of the cosmic patterns of the race, expressed and accepted in the chants and legends repeated again and again. The race was the crux, the only living entity. The individual was nothing, but the communality was all, from which sprang the giving away and exchanging of children, the incestuous intermarriages of the chiefs, and the natural commingling of living things—dogs, chickens, pigs, and people, all huddled in the dark, windowless grass huts.

Altogether it was a society built on a fragile frame, and carrying as time went by a steadily heavier weight of social strain. Like similar societies vegetating in involuted isolation, it contained the seeds of its own destruction, ready to burst open at the first touch of foreign hands, some seeds to blossom forth in new guise, others to crumble into nothingness.

The foreign hands came to their shores in wondrous vessels—thought at first by the natives to be moving islands—beginning in 1778 with Captain James Cook, who was received as an incarnation of Lono upon his arrival during the *makahiki* festival season and was later killed in a banal fight between English sailors and Hawaiians, almost as a harbinger of the day when the Hawaiians would destroy all their gods.

After Cook, other explorers and sea captains came: Vancouver with cattle, the seeds of strange plants, and sound advice for the native rulers; other Englishmen like Portlock and Dixon, who wrote accounts of their dealings in the newly discovered land; Russian adventurers and seafarers like Kotzebue and Golovnin; seamen who became teachers and confidants of kings and high chiefs, such as John Young and Isaac Davis; and within a score of years hundreds of sailors, deserters, derelicts, and intriguers, who brought a grab bag of civilization's benefits and baubles to a people at first bewildered by what was happening to them and then growingly demoralized.

The *ali'i* avidly sought the material goods of the newcomers, seeing in their guns, ships, horses, and metals new means for increasing their strength in relation to rival chiefs. But as their material power grew, their implicit faith in their own ways and beliefs, and also the faith of the commoners, began to weaken as it became clear that it was the *haole*, or foreigners, who possessed the greater mana. The foreigners violated the taboos with impunity and imposed their will more fully each day. For the *ali'i* the sacral strand that had bound them to the gods was being broken. They no longer felt themselves to be sacrosanct in the same way. Now their claim to high status and respect lay increasingly in aping foreign ways, adopting *haole* dress and manners, and obtaining foreign wares for prestige and conspicuous consumption. The old gods were dying.

In the second decade of the nineteenth century—barely thirty years after the coming of Cook—social disintegration became more pronounced. Hawaiians began to violate the *kapu* system with increasing frequency, and finally in 1819 the crisis came with the death of Kamehameha the Great. Many of the old customs were carried out at his funeral, the bones were hidden, and widespread mourning occurred, but no human sacrifice was allowed either during his final illness or as part of the funeral ceremonies. Hawaii was now deprived of a leader of stature, a man who had guided the unsure people of the islands partway across the immense chasm that separated the Stone Age of thirty years earlier from the embryonic nation that was coming into being.

The succeeding ruler, young Liholiho (reigned 1819–24), was inexperienced and indecisive. He shared power with the queen regent, Kaahumanu, favorite wife of the deceased Kamehameha, and pressure from her and other female chiefs to abandon the forms of *kapu* that weighed most heavily on women became pronounced. For a time Liholiho hesitated; he had been named caretaker of the gods and had the *kapu* of the temples. But he overcame his vacillation dramatically in a public ceremony in November 1819 by ostentatiously sitting with the women at a banquet in Kailua, on the island of Hawaii, and thus breaking the taboo that had prevented men and women from eating together. This "free eating" (*ai noa*) effectively symbolized the end of the *kapu* system. Although there was an abortive attempt at a coup

Statue of the deity Ku in the City of Refuge, Honaunau, Hawaii.

Hawaiian *kahuna,* or priest. (Photo courtesy of the Archives of Hawaii)

...ove: Coat of arms of the Kingdom of Hawaii on the gate of the Royal ...ausoleum, Honolulu. *Right:* Statue of Kamehameha the Great, unifier ...f the islands, Hawi, Hawaii.

...trance to Hale o Keawe, mausoleum of the high chiefs of ... island of Hawaii, City of Refuge, Honaunau, Hawaii.

The first Catholic church in the island of Hawaii, Puna. (Photo courtesy of the Archives of Hawaii)

Etching of Kahikuonalani Church, Ewa, Oahu, as it looked in 1851. (Photo courtesy of the Mission Houses Museum, Honolulu)

'elehu Chapel, Maui, the first Mormon church in Hawaii, as it looked c. 1852. (Photo courtesy of the Archives of Hawaii)

View of the Mission-house and Chapel, in Honoruru. (Oahu.)

Etching of the Mission House and chapel, Honolulu, c. 1822, with Diamond Head in the background. (Photo courtesy of the Mission Houses Museum, Honolulu)

Above and opposite page: Kawaiahao Church, Honolulu (completed 1842), as it appeared in 1885 (above), with Waikiki and Diamond Head in the background, and as it is today. (Monochrome photo courtesy of the Archives of Hawaii)

Waiohinu Church, Hawaii. (Photo courtesy of the Archives of Hawaii)

Mission House, Honolulu (built 1821–28), the home of the American Congregationalist missionaries who built nearby Kawaiahao Church.

Imiola Congregational Church, Waimea, Hawaii.

Kalihi Mormon Chapel, Honolulu, at
the time of its dedication in 1924.
(Photo courtesy of the Archives of Hawaii)

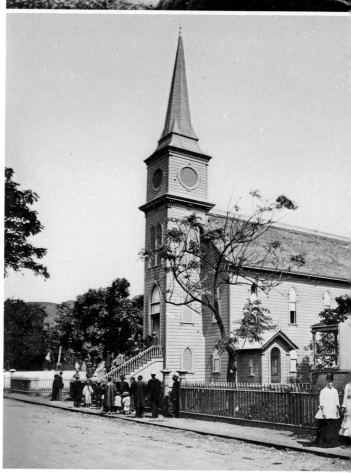

Chinese Christian Church, Honolulu. (Photo
courtesy of the Archives of Hawaii)

Hongwanji Mission on Fort Street, Honolulu. (Photo courtesy of the Archives of Hawaii)

Kalahikiola Congregational Church, near Hawi, Hawaii.

Baldwin House, home of American Congregationalist missionary Dwight Baldwin, Lahaina, Maui.

Mokuaikaua Church, Kailua, Hawaii (completed 1837).

Central Union Church, Honolulu, as it looked in 1912. (Photo courtesy of the Mission Houses Museum, Honolulu

Kaumakapili Church, Honolulu, as it looked in 1888. Procathedral of Saint Andrew's Cathedral, Honolulu, as it
(Photo courtesy of the Archives of Hawaii) appeared in 1866. (Photo courtesy of the Archives of Hawaii)

Central Union Church, Honolulu, as it is today.

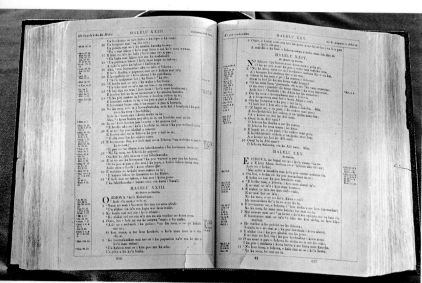

Hawaiian-language Bible in Hui Aloha Congregational
Church, Keanae, Maui.

Hui Aloha Congregational Church, Keanae, Maui.

Exterior and interior of Wananalua Congregational Church, Hana, Maui.

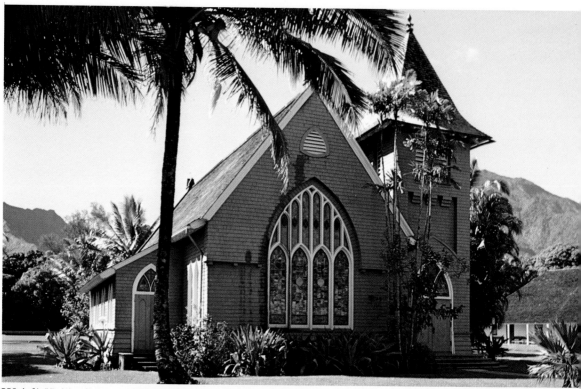

Waioli Hui'ia Congregational Church, Hanalei, Kauai.

Waioli Mission House, Hanalei, Kauai.

Stained-glass window of Waioli Hui'ia Congregational Church, Hanalei, Kau

"Foreign Church," built by American Congregationalist missionaries, Waimea, Kauai.

by a coterie of chiefs headed by a cousin of Liholiho who had custody
of the war god, Ku, it failed and the entire struggle was over almost
at once. The astonishing spectacle was then seen of the *kahuna* themselves destroying idols and temples in an orgy of emotional self-
mortification and abasement. The *ali'i*, who had profited so much from
the social system as a whole, saw the collapse of the *kapu* restrictions
with indifference. They were more concerned with their new commercial interests, their share in the lucrative sandalwood trade, and the
profitability of their contacts with foreign merchants.

For a brief period, beginning in the autumn of 1819, Hawaii became
something unique in human history: a land in limbo, without any formal, organized religion. The breakdown of the elaborate socio-reli-
gious system of past ages had brought a sudden and total collapse of
belief and left a yawning spiritual vacuum. The old gods were indeed
dead, but within a few months a new faith was on the way.

2

The Companies of
the Congregation

"YOU ARE TO AIM AT NOTHING SHORT of covering those islands with fruitful fields and pleasant dwellings, and schools and churches; of raising up the whole people to an elevated state of Christian civilization. . . ." Fortified by these instructions from the Prudential Committee of the American Board of Commissioners for Foreign Missions, seven evangelical missionaries and their wives, accompanied by three Hawaiian youths who had studied at the Foreign Mission School in Connecticut—a group of seventeen people in all—set sail from Boston in the autumn of 1819. They changed the course of Hawaiian history and shaped a nation out of the clay of a still primitive society beginning to come apart under the impact of its first meeting with the outside world.

The group was wholly ignorant of how timely its coming would be. It had left New England on the Thaddeus only a few weeks before the

Hawaiian chiefs had broken the taboos and cast aside their idols, and it arrived in the early spring of 1820 to find a people dazzled but demoralized by the new world into which they were being daily more closely drawn and, however unconsciously, ready to be led along new spiritual paths.

Landing at Kailua in early April, the missionaries were received, with a thoroughly Hawaiian blend of curiosity, dilatory palaver, and politeness, by the young king, his chief minister, and his wife and half-sister, Kamamalu. The French and British personal advisers to Liholiho, who had their own private and national interests to guard, were cool to the Americans, and while the sovereign and his immediate retinue were friendly, the thought of the demands of a new religion held little immediate appeal to those, especially the women, who were enjoying their new-found freedom from the *kapu* system.

What won the day were the practical arts the missionaries commanded. Many of the nobility were eager to learn the *palapala*, the mysterious letters of the foreigners, and the skill of the company's physician was deemed so desirable that he was required to stay behind, along with part of the company, with the king and his court at Kailua when the missionaries after more than a week of discussion received permission for part of their group to establish a station in the main port of Honolulu, something they felt to be vital to the success of their enterprise.

There, in a frowzy village of grass shacks and grog shops cluttering a barren, dusty plain, the churchmen settled in the midst of some of their own Yankee kin. But the New England seafaring captains, traders, and cargo agents who had preceded them were infected with another fever, that of the sandalwood trade. They paid the islanders to bring the fragrant logs down from the mountains, they loaded the wood on board ships already heavy with fur pelts from northwest America, and they cleared for Canton, where the precious cargo was exchanged for Chinese teas, silks, and porcelain. Late in his lifetime, Kamehameha the Great had vainly tried to stem the frenzy of tree-cutting, but in the immediate years after his death the common people were driven to exhaustion and the hills denuded by chiefs only too willing to trade their resources for Spanish dollars and foreign wares.

At the beginning, the captains and merchants looked indifferently upon the newcomers, little realizing that the preaching and teaching the latter proposed to undertake would soon prove to be an even headier concoction for many Hawaiians than the products of their own rum casks, and that the interests of the two groups would inevitably clash. So the small group set to work in the summer of 1820 to carry out its mission. The missionaries never forgot that the salvation of the heathen and their redemption from sin was the ultimate goal, but the practicalities of their situation made it necessary to give priority to printing, to instructing the natives in reading, and in the first instance to teaching themselves the Hawaiian language.

At first glance more unlikely candidates for attaining a degree of harmonious influence over the gentle, indulgent, but often excitable Hawaiians could hardly be imagined. Yet, in the adoption which followed—and it was precisely that kind of family relationship which grew up—the unbending strength of the missionaries and the very austerity of their belief and conduct gave birth to a respect on the part of the Hawaiians that more than anything else made success possible during the following two decades. The seriousness of the mission staff and their humble devotion to their daily tasks impressed many of the chiefs. The Hawaiians gradually came to realize that these men were another breed, quite separate from most of the flotsam clogging the port of Honolulu. They had a different virtue, a new kind of mana.

At first this feeling was unspoken, and in a way even unfelt, by Hawaiians. To the missionaries the primary purpose of the venture was the *pule*, the preaching of the word of God and the saving of souls. To the Hawaiians at first the secular *palapala*, the teaching of reading and writing, which was only a means to a higher end in the eyes of the evangelists, was something that conferred status, just as the goods and guns and coins of the *haole* traders did. And in 1822 Liholiho was still insisting that the missionaries must first learn Hawaiian well, in order to be able to put the words of his tongue into writing that he could see and admire; later he would tell his people to worship their God.

Under the surface, however, a longing for spiritual guidance was beginning to stir. Almost all the written material available in the first years for instructional use was religious: sermons from the Bible, hymn books, religious homilies, and finally the New Testament and then the entire Bible printed in Hawaiian. As the printed words seeped into the consciousness of the chiefs and the common people alike, the underlying meaning of these words and something of the spirit that had fashioned them also entered the minds and hearts of the students.

There were motifs that were not entirely unfamiliar, and many concepts struck echoes in the Hawaiian soul, only a few years removed from longstanding and well-understood pagan practice. Iehova, the God of the new teachers, was a stern and awesome figure; disobedience of his commands brought terrible punishment, different in form but similar in concept to those of the ancient gods. Moreover, the imported faith had its taboos, which the new priestly class insisted must be carefully kept; the ban put on card playing, gambling, and drinking might well vex the *ali'i*, who had rapidly become fond of such diversions, but it could also be understood in the light of ancient edicts forbidding the eating of designated foods or the drinking of narcotic *awa* liquor in certain seasons. There had always been forbidden pleasures; it was only that the new *kapu* were different from the old. A sympathetic bond was formed, too, as the Hawaiians learned that their daring destruction of their own gods and temples had been a noble and righteous act that gained them favor in the eyes of God and hence of the missionaries. And ultimately, the simple, bare altars of the first mission churches implicitly reassured the Hawaiians that the old idols were gone never to return.

If there were any lingering doubts to that effect in Hawaiian minds, they were dispelled by the dramatic pilgrimage of the high chief Kapiolani to the brink of the firepit at the volcano Kilauea on the island of Hawaii just before Christmas in 1824. She had earlier been converted to Christianity and was a pious student of the new religion. In order to discredit certain priestesses who had been reviving the cult of Pele, goddess of fire and destruction, Kapiolani walked the breadth of the island of Hawaii and ordered a religious service to be held at the edge of the Halemaumau crater of Kilauea, formerly believed to be the home of Pele. There she uttered her famous words "Iehovah is my God, He kindled these fires, I fear not Pele," ate *ohelo* berries, sacred to the goddess but *kapu* for women, threw stones into the crater, and remained unscathed in the midst of general rejoicing and prayer.

Important changes in the religious scene in Hawaii came after the young Liholiho and his queen died, while visiting London in 1824, as the result of an attack of measles. The *kuhina nui* or chief adviser, Kaahumanu, assumed authority as regent and ruled for eight years during the boyhood of Kamehameha III (reigned 1825–54). In her later years she came to give enthusiastic support to the new religion, and after having been admitted to the church in 1825, proclaimed laws establishing monogamy, enjoining the observance of the Sabbath, and prohibiting gaming and lewdness of all kinds. Her patronage, along with that of other great female chiefs, such as Keopuolani and Kapiolani, and later that of Kinau, the sister of Kamehameha III, who was appointed regent and chief minister upon the death of Kaahumanu in 1832, was crucial not merely in furthering the enterprise of the Congregational missions, but for the whole movement of Christianizing the Hawaiian nation.

As support from the rulers and chiefs firmed in the years after 1820, the missionaries deployed their endeavors in a number of fields, in each of which they left a lasting imprint; among the most noteworthy were architecture, language, education, and music.

The need for suitable quarters for the members of the First Company on Oahu was felt from the day of their arrival, and after much pleading they obtained land just east of Honolulu village, near the path that led to Waikiki. Having obtained permission from Liholiho to stay on beyond the original one-year term of residence granted them, in 1821 they built there a two-story frame house, the first wooden dwelling in the Hawaiian islands. This structure was supplemented the following year by a printing house, and in 1828 the ensemble was completed by a combined residence and storehouse made of coral blocks cut from the nearby reef. The complex, known as the Mission Houses, stands today as a historical monument in downtown Honolulu at one end of the Civic Center.

In the first weeks and months, the earliest dwelling served as home, school, office, and church at the same time. Services were held on Sunday in the same rooms where classes met during the week, until a church could be built later in the year. Filled with mahogany chests, four-poster beds, walnut furniture, and leather-bound books, and brightened by colorful quilts and snow-white curtains, the houses brought a crisp breath of early America to the sun-drenched tropical plain on which they stood as beacons pointing to a new life.

Other mission houses that blended the tidiness and simplicity of New England homes with tropical surroundings were soon constructed on other islands. The beautiful Waioli Mission House at Hanalei on the island of Kauai is a delightful example of such a marriage, and Baldwin House at Lahaina on Maui is equally redolent with memories of the lives and times of the early missionaries.

The missionaries built not only for themselves but for their new

HAWAII AND ITS GODS

congregations as well. Compelled at first to hold open-air services for the thousands of curious Hawaiians who came to hear the gospel, partly at the exhortation of newly pious chiefs but also because the Sabbath was now a day of rest in which a pleasant distraction could be found in listening to the fervent declamations of the ministers, the missionaries were eager to build solid and worthy houses of God as soon as possible.

In this desire they were aided by the ardor of some of the chiefly converts. At Kailua on Hawaii, where the original landing had been made and where a small temporary church had been built after the establishment of the mission in 1820, Governor Kuakini attempted to buy his baptism by having a handsome church built for the new religion. He sent his subjects to the mountains to cut timber and bear it to the village, and he oversaw personally the long and tedious work of construction. Finally in 1837, in the same year that saw his own elegant frame house take shape in Kailua town, the present church of Mokuaikaua was dedicated: a majestic structure of whitewashed lava rocks cemented together with mortar made from coral taken from the nearby harbor. With its tapering spire towering over the town even now and dominating it in spirit and in substance, Mokuaikaua is the oldest continuously used Christian church in the islands.

The greatest monument to the efforts of the Congregational companies, however, is probably the noble church they erected in Honolulu over a period of five years and which was opened for worship in July 1842. Kawaiahao, the Stone Church, which stands adjacent to the Mission Houses and facing Palace Square, was conceived and designed by the leader of the First Company, the assiduous and visionary Hiram Bingham, and was built on land given by Kamehameha III. Bingham himself left the islands in 1840 and never saw the completion of his project. From its inception it has been at the center of Hawaiian history and faith. Only a year after its dedication, in July 1843, it was the scene of a dramatic thanksgiving reunion celebrating the restoration of Hawaiian sovereignty to the rulers of Hawaii by Admiral Thomas, commander in chief of the British navy in the Pacific, after it had been usurped by force a few months earlier by another British commander. It was on this occasion that Kamehameha III, in a speech whose full text has been lost, is said to have used the expression that later became the phrase used on the coat of arms of the kingdom and is now used as the official motto of the State of Hawaii: *Ua mau ke ea o ka aina i ka pono* (The life of the land lives in righteousness).

Built of buff-colored coral blocks, the church has dignified proportions and a simple interior surmounted by a balcony overlooking the former Royal Pew, a concession granted by Kamehameha III during the planning of the construction. Kawaiahao has been the scene of coronations, funerals, and innumerable state ceremonies. For two decades after its dedication, until the chapel of the Royal Mausoleum was built in the Nuuanu Valley above Honolulu, it was the worshiping place of the monarchs of Hawaii. Gradually it became a kind of national shrine, transcending sectarian differences, and today it still holds a secure place in the hearts of Hawaiians of all faiths, which entitles it to be called, as it so often is, the Westminster Abbey of Hawaii.

The endeavors of the missionaries in language and education were also of prime importance; indeed, they were essential to the central mission of saving Hawaiian souls. It is not often realized how arduous was the task of learning an unwritten language like Hawaiian, and how painstaking was the process of standardizing it and putting it on paper. And this preliminary and purely linguistic work was only the prelude to translating the words of Jesus and the writings of the Hebrew prophets into a tongue where the abstract concepts of Christian thought and civilization were largely absent.

In January 1822 the Mission Printing House in Honolulu turned out its first product, an English spelling book, and over the next few years a growing stream of school primers, religious pamphlets, and hymnals issued forth. As fast as their knowledge of Hawaiian permitted, the missionaries undertook the task of translating the Bible. The New Testament was completed by 1832, and seven years later the entire Bible had been printed in Hawaiian. In 1834 a second printing plant was founded at the school at Lahainaluna on Maui. Textbooks were printed there and in that same year the first Hawaiian newspaper, *Ka Lama Hawaii*, appeared.

Although schools were established in the first months after the arrival of the First Company, education took hold slowly. Learning to read in an alien tongue through the medium of a speller and a catechism was a laborious task for Hawaiians, and it was not until they saw the words of their own language in print that interest became widespread. It was the chiefs who responded first, for they had wisely been catered to in the expectation that progress would spread downward, by precept and example, from noble to commoner. At the end of 1824 more than 2,000 pupils were enrolled; by 1828 this figure had risen to 37,000, and by 1832 there were already 52,000 students, at least one-third of the population. These were adults in the main, although the education of children was increasingly emphasized after the pressing task of giving elementary instruction in reading and civics to the older generation was well under way. In the best Hawaiian manner, the people turned the examination (*hoike*) into a gala festival, to which they came replete with feather leis and fancy adornments as well as slates; all were summoned to the meeting house by the blowing of a conch.

Nor did the missionaries neglect the power that the charms of music had to instill piety in the breasts of their flock. The end result may not have been what they imagined when they first taught the unfamiliar sounds of the diatonic scale and its strange polyphony to ears accustomed only to a repetitive chanting on alternating notes. But from the hymns and the choir singing that issued from the church services there came the new voice of Hawaii. This was an entirely distinctive pattern of sounds and rhythms nurtured by church music, embellished by the guitars of imported Mexican *paniolo* cowboys and the ukuleles brought later by immigrant Portuguese, and Hawaiianized by the scores of gifted musicians and composers found among both royalty and ordinary Hawaiians in succeeding years and decades.

In this field, too, Hiram Bingham applied himself with his usual zeal, and in 1837 his *Hawaiian Hymns and Music* was published. The missionaries introduced the word *himeni* (from "hymn") into the language to differentiate their sacred music from the *mele* and *oli* chants of the pagan period; the word was taken up by Hawaiians and passed into general use with the meaning of any song, secular or religious, that is not to be danced to, as distinguished from the *hula*.

It is not unfair to say in perspective that the missionaries had literally brought a nation into being and given it a definitive form, a stamp that it would always keep a good part of. With generosity and devotion as they understood them, the men and women of the Companies of God endowed their second home as best they could with the arts and sciences of their time. But this being so, in their desire to ensure that their adopted land be soundly guided they were unable to resist the temptation to enter into the most dangerous arena of all, that of politics. They did this, again, with perhaps the best of intentions from their strict and severe viewpoint, but the step was one that would eventually turn many men, foreign and native, against them, and in the end bring the shadow of a bitter schism to the land and people they cherished.

The missionary group had had considerable indirect political influence from the earliest years of settlement, of course, especially after Kaahumanu formally endorsed their views in 1824. As the complications of international politics multiplied in the ensuing decade, the Reverend William Richards, a member of the Second Company serving in Lahaina, left the mission to become unofficial chaplain, teacher, and translator to Kamehameha III. He lectured to the chiefs and the king on the art of political economy, and it was he who helped shape the Declaration of Rights of 1839, which was inserted as a preamble to the constitution that was proclaimed the following year: "God hath made of one blood all nations of men, to dwell on the face of the earth in unity and blessedness. God has also bestowed certain rights alike on all men, and all chiefs, and all people of all lands.

"These are some of the rights which He has given alike to every man and every chief, life, limb, liberty, the labor of his hands, and productions of his mind. . . ."

There were others who entered government service and occupied prominent places in the public eye. One such was Dr. Gerrit Judd, missionary and doctor, and a member of the Third Company. Dr. Judd continued Richards's work and, beginning in 1842, undertook with remarkable success the overwhelming task of organizing a functioning, modern government. Through the next several years, Judd was the moving spirit behind the Organic Act, the great Mahele land reform of 1848, the constitution of 1852, and innumerable other works of government and administration. At the beginning of his career he was forced to rely heavily on foreigners for official posts because of the insufficient quantity of Hawaiian talent—with consequent native resentment. Later, his wish to place restrictions on land sales to non-Hawaiians alienated white men, and he was consequently denounced by Hawaiian and *haole* alike as the "Missionary in the Palace." His presence, and that of other foreigners around him, at the helm of state affairs brought into the open for the first time a bitterness felt by many Hawaiians as they sensed that power was slipping away from them in their own land.

The twelfth and last of the companies arrived in 1848, and somewhere about that time the history that they had played so large a part in writing pauses. Conversions to Christianity, which were slow at first and had been deliberately discouraged by the missionaries on the grounds that few Hawaiians were sufficiently aware of the commitment necessary for baptism, grew rapidly during the "Great Revival" of 1837–40, especially in parishes on the island of Hawaii led by energetic pastors like Lorenzo Lyons at Waimea and Titus Coan in Hilo. During those three years nearly twenty thousand Hawaiians were received into the church. Many of the conversions were emotional and short-lived; numbers of the baptized drifted away, and some missionaries feared that such backsliding would undo the patient work of previous years.

But all in all, that was not so. By 1840 it was clear that Hawaii was a Christian nation, in its roots as well as in its constitution, which declared "that no law shall be enacted which is at variance with the word of the Lord Jehovah, or at variance with the general spirit of His word." Thousands of Hawaiians could read and write their own language; the nation was becoming literate; books and newspapers and journals were being widely printed. Orderly government and succession had been insured, and men had guarantees equal to those in the supposedly most advanced countries of Europe and America. The transformation wrought in the sixty-odd years since the arrival of Cook was truly prodigious, and although scattered reinforcements and replacements for the missionaries trickled out to Hawaii until 1894, the mission had in effect been satisfactorily completed before midcentury. The missionaries had labored in the love of God as they understood him, and they had kept full faith.

Nevertheless, the shadows of religious conflict among Christians, which had appeared earlier, were darkening late in the fourth decade of the century, and although Hawaii was generally recognized to be a Christian country at that time, it was not yet certain which form of Christianity would predominate.

3

The Apostolic Mission

THE STRUGGLE OF THE Roman Catholic missionaries to gain recognition, respectability, and the right to preach their concept of the true faith in the face of what they felt to be the twin evils of paganism and Calvinism was longer and more bitter than that of their Protestant predecessors. In good part their misfortunes stemmed from the very fact they had made an untimely late arrival on the scene, just after Kaahumanu and other paramount chiefs had become committed to the teachings of the Congregational mission of Bingham and his companions. For the Catholic priests brought a confusingly different interpretation of the new religion to the Hawaiians, who had finally accepted, after some doubts, the verity of the New England version. In fact, it must have seemed to many of the chiefs that Catholicism was an altogether different faith, with a profusion of strange sacraments and its own idols and images. And to compound the problem, the difficulties

of the Catholics in the first twenty years after their arrival were augmented by the vagaries of history and the complications of power
politics arising in Europe and casting their shadow over the Pacific.

The initial cloud upon the presence of the Roman Catholics in Hawaii lay in the manner of their coming. Although there were a few
individuals among the earliest foreigners resident in the islands who
professed the faith quietly, the first Catholic priests arrived on the
French warship Uranie when it visited Hawaii in August 1819. The
vessel carried a company of French explorers and scientists under the
command of Louis de Freycinet, who left a detailed account of his
voyage, made just as the *kapu* system was on the point of breaking
down. A few baptisms of high officials appear to have been made at
that time, but since the Hawaiians knew little of Christianity and had
no time to receive catechism during the brief visit of the corvette, it is
likely that these were acts of political artifice on the part of many of
the participants in the baptismal ceremonies.

De Freycinet reassured his cautious hosts about French intentions,
proclaimed the disinterested friendship of his government for the
Hawaiian kingdom and its understanding of Hawaiian ties with Great
Britain, and then went his way. But over the next three decades Hawaii
was visited by a number of French gunboats whose captains bullied the
native authorities and forced them to capitulate to often extravagant
demands, among which the right of Catholic clergy to reside and teach
on a footing of equality with other missionaries was perhaps the least
objectionable. If this demand had certain political overtones, it was also
a point of honor about which the French government had strong feelings. But although the French insistence on equal religious opportunity
was understandable—and it was even to the Protestant missionaries,
who disapproved wholeheartedly of Romans and their ways but de-
fended their right to free speech—to the Hawaiian leaders the linking
of religious and political pressures filled them with misgivings about
the new brand of the faith and with suspicions about the underlying
motives of those who protected it. It was a long time before these
feelings of mistrust were laid to rest.

Probably the most important arrival for the later development of
the Catholic presence in Hawaii was a young French adventurer, Jean
Rives, one of the first foreigners to reside in the islands. He attached
himself at an early age to Liholiho, and ultimately became interpreter,
companion, and secretary to the king. Rives accompanied the young

monarch to England during his voyage in 1823–24, but after the death of the king in London he fell out of favor with the remainder of the royal party. His ambitions appear to have been both commercial and religious, and he found fertile ground in France for both aspects of his endeavors. A conservative and clerical regime, renewed Catholic missionary zeal, and an expansionist policy in colonial affairs all combined to create in France at that time an atmosphere propitious for arranging a commercial enterprise that aimed at the establishment of an agricultural settler colony and a Catholic mission in the Hawaiian islands simultaneously.

Rives had promised to use his influence on behalf of all parties to the venture, but while in California en route back to Hawaii from Europe it was learned that he had fallen out of favor with Kaahumanu and that the nobles were now under the influence of the American missionaries. Rives himself did not return to Hawaii, but the Comète, carrying three priests and three other lay members of the mission, arrived in Honolulu in July 1827. The small group landed without permission and the Hawaiian authorities ordered the captain of the vessel to remove them from Hawaiian soil, but the Comète sailed without reboarding the party. In Hawaiian fashion, the ban placed on their entry was not enforced, and the small band of missionaries settled in, built a house, and in 1828 opened a chapel for public worship. The agricultural colony soon failed, but the missionaries stayed on, learned something of the language, and by the middle of the following year had made a few score converts among the populace. The Catholic faith was implanted shakily but definitely in Hawaii.

The Catholics had the support of the governor of Oahu, Boki, who had been baptized a Catholic and was opposed to the growing dominance of Kaahumanu. Nevertheless, his influence was not sufficient to protect them indefinitely, and in August 1829 an edict was issued ordering Hawaiians to desist from attending Catholic services. The following January the priests were forbidden to teach Catholicism, but they refused to obey. The persecution of local converts continued through 1830, after a ship carrying Governor Boki was lost at sea while engaged in the sandalwood trade. Finally, in January 1831, an order of banishment was issued; but the priests demurred and once again it was not enforced until the chiefs provided their own vessel and forcibly deported the two remaining fathers to Mexican California. There they resided at Mission San Gabriel, outside Los Angeles, until they might return to Hawaii.

After the expulsion of the priests, persecution of native converts diminished for several years, but the Catholic problem soon flared anew. In 1833 the Propaganda Fide (Society for the Propagation of the Faith) had entrusted the Apostolic Vicariate in the Eastern Pacific to the Order of the Sacred Hearts. It then confirmed Father Bachelot, one of the two expelled fathers, as Apostolic Prefect of the Hawaiian region within that area. In 1836 another priest, a British subject, Father Walsh, arrived in Honolulu under the sponsorship of the order. He, too, was directed to leave Hawaiian soil, but his banishment was prevented by the arrival of another French warship, the Bonite, whose captain impressed upon local authorities the extent of French power and his willingness to see it used to protect French interests throughout the world. Once again Catholic interests were assumed to coincide with French interests, and once again the chiefs bowed as gracefully as possible to gunboat diplomacy. Yet both sides held fast to their principles: while allowing Father Walsh to stay, the Hawaiian government ordered him not to proselytize among its subjects; and the good father, holding divine command in higher esteem, felt no compunction about converting and baptizing a number of Hawaiians.

The situation was soon exacerbated by the return of the expelled priests, Fathers Bachelot and Short, in April 1837. The usual round of proclamatory expulsion, defiance, confrontation, and capitulation by the Hawaiian authorities began again. After diplomatic incidents including the seizure of a foreign vessel and the burning of the British flag, the two priests were formally escorted ashore by French and British consuls and the captains of warships of the two countries. An impasse now resulted: the Catholic fathers could stay, but written guarantees were given that they would leave at the first opportunity.

Later in the same year still other priests arrived, including Father Maigret, who was eventually to found and lead the Catholic mission in Hawaii for a number of years. In late November, Bachelot and Maigret were forced to leave on the schooner Notre Dame de Paix, which had been purchased by the mission; Father Short had already left, and only a recently ordained priest who was not publicly known to be so, Father Murphy, remained to carry on covert missionary work. At this juncture, in December 1837, Kamehameha III issued a formal edict,

Interior of Saint Benedict's Catholic Church, Honaunau, Haw.
one of the Kona coast's "painted churches." *Trompe-l'oeil* painti
represents the transept and apse of the cathedral of Burgos, Spa

"An Ordinance Rejecting the Catholic Religion," which stated in part: "Therefore, I, with my chiefs, forbid . . . that anyone should teach the peculiarities of the Pope's religion, nor shall it be allowed to anyone who teaches those doctrines or those peculiarities to reside in this kingdom; nor shall the ceremonies be exhibited in our kingdom, nor shall anyone teaching its peculiarities or its faith be permitted to land on these shores; for it is not proper that two religions be found in this small kingdom. Therefore we utterly refuse to allow anyone to teach those peculiarities in any manner whatsoever. We moreover prohibit all vessels whatsoever from bringing any teacher of that religion into this kingdom."

The royal ordinance and the last expulsion of priests finally provoked the full wrath of the French government, which not only considered itself the defender of the faith but held that the acts of the Hawaiian government were in violation of the convention signed that very summer between France and Hawaii, under the terms of which French subjects could come and go freely in the Sandwich Islands, as the archipelago was then known, on a most-favored-nation basis, while equal rights were given to Hawaiian subjects on French territory.

In consequence, orders were dispatched to Captain Laplace of the frigate Artemise in the summer of 1838, which he received early the following year in Australia. He was to sail to both the Society Islands and the Sandwich Islands—in the former the French feared British commercial and political influence, just as they distrusted American activities in the latter—and "to make it well understood that it will be altogether to the advantage of the chiefs of those islands of the Ocean to conduct themselves in such a manner as not to incur the wrath of France. You will exact, if necessary with all the force that is yours to use, complete reparation for the wrongs which have been committed, and you will not quit those places until you have left in all minds a solid and lasting impression."

The threat of reprisals appears to have had its effect. In June 1839 the king gave oral instructions that no punishment be visited upon those practicing the Catholic faith. In part this change of policy may have been made possible by the death of the virulently anti-Catholic regent, Kinau, in April 1839; and in part it may have been influenced by the pleadings of American missionaries for a spirit of tolerance and by the warnings of British and other naval officers that only a policy of religious tolerance could prevail over the long term. But in the main

Interior and exterior of Saint Benedict's Catholic
Church, Honaunau, Hawaii.

Saint Michael's Catholic Church, Kailua, Hawaii.

Statue of the Virgin Mary in a roadside
grotto near Hana, Maui.

Opposite page: Saint Peter's Catholic
Church, near Kahaluu, Hawaii.

Saint Joseph's Catholic Church, near Kamalo, Molokai, built by Father Damien 1874–76.

Statue of Father Damien at the State Capitol, Honolulu.

Stations of the cross by Jean Charlot in Saint Sylvester's Catholic Church, Kilauea, Kauai.

Overleaf: Sacred Hearts Catholic Church, Hawi, Hawaii.

Our Lady Queen of Angels Catholic Church, popularly known as the Octagonal Church, near Kula, Maui.

Altar of Our Queen of Angels Catholic Church.

Interior of Saint Raphael's Catholic Church, Koloa, Kauai.

Punchbowl Holy Ghost Church, Honolulu, a relic of the time when
many Portuguese immigrants lived on Punchbowl's slop

Interior of the Cathedral of Our Lady of Peace, Honolulu (completed 1843) (Photo by Jean-Paul Chaine)

Overleaf: Mormon Temple, Laie, Oahu, the religious center in Hawaii of the Church of Jesus Christ of Latter-day Saints.

THE CHURCH OF

Saint Andrew's Cathedral, Honolulu, headquarters
of the Episcopal church in Hawaii.

TO THE GLORY OF GOD AND IN LOVING MEMORY OF
ELIZABETH MITCHELL ADAMS · DEC 31 1841-OCT 16 19

Above and opposite page: German Lutheran Church, Lihue, Kauai (completed 1884).

Chapel of the Royal Mausoleum, Honolulu (completed 1865).

it undoubtedly stemmed from information reaching Hawaii in the spring of that year about the exaction of an indemnity and an apology from and the forced signing of a treaty by the queen of Tahiti, in the Society Islands; and by the disquieting news that a French squadron would soon be sent to the Hawaiian Islands for the same purposes.

The oral proclamation of religious tolerance preceded the French visit by about one month, but it did not prevent the visit, nor did it allow the Hawaiian government to escape the humiliation of an ultimatum and a complete capitulation. The Artemise arrived in Honolulu on July 9, 1839, and a manifesto containing five demands was presented to the king by Laplace. It required that the Catholic faith be freely taught throughout the islands; that a site for a church of the Catholic faith be given by the Hawaiian government; that all Catholics imprisoned for religious reasons be freed at once; that the king deposit a sum of money guaranteeing future behavior toward France and French nationals; and that a public ceremony be carried out involving a salute to the French flag. The treaty was signed within three days on behalf of the king, and the money was hastily raised from local merchants. The punishment was completed the following Sunday, when 180 French military men and officers came ashore and attended a mass celebrated by Father Walsh on royal property. After twenty years of harassment the Catholic church had been firmly established in Hawaii by persistence and force of arms.

After the persecution came to an end the real work of building the Catholic church in Hawaii began at several levels. The most important psychological consideration in the beginning was the building of a cathedral to symbolize the Catholic presence formally. For this purpose Bishop Rouchouze, who had directed the mission from his headquarters in Mangareva, near Tahiti, went to Honolulu in 1840. On July 9 of that year—the first anniversary of the arrival of the Artemise, and the feast day of Our Lady of Peace—he broke ground for the construction of the new cathedral to be named in her honor. Bishop Rouchouze was lost at sea after leaving Hawaii early the following year, and was succeeded by Father Maigret, who should be looked on as the true founder of the church in Hawaii. Consecrated as bishop in 1847, he was the mainstay of Catholic work and faith for nearly three decades thereafter.

Work on the Cathedral of Our Lady of Peace proceeded under his direction and was completed in August 1843, a year after Kawaiahao was opened for services. The spirit of the two leading churches of Honolulu could not have been more dissimilar, nor their physical appearance more different. The ecumenical, Latin flavor of the Catholic edifice contrasted sharply with the spare simplicity of the Congregational church. The cathedral's tower clock had been brought from a church of the Sacred Hearts in Chile; the tower bells, installed in 1853, came from France, and the altar of Carrara marble from Italy. The first *kiawe* tree, parent of all others in Hawaii, sprang from a seed brought from the Royal Conservatory in Paris; the tree stands in the courtyard alongside a statue of Our Lady of Peace, erected for the centennial observance of the founding of the mission, with inscriptions in French, English, Portuguese, and Hawaiian. There, in 1864, Father Damien, minister to the lepers, celebrated his first mass.

The cathedral was of course only the formal facade; the heart of mission activity was conversion, and new missionaries and lay helpers arrived to pursue the task of instructing and baptizing. By the end of 1840 it was estimated that the number of baptisms on Oahu had risen to some two thousand. Within a year, missionary work had been extended to the islands of Hawaii and Kauai, and by 1846 to Maui. The celebrated Virgin of the Roadside and the Cross, dedicated to the first Hawaiian convert in East Maui, is evidence of the Catholic fervor that swept that island in the 1840s. By 1853 a census of the Catholic population of all the islands showed 11,401 adherents out of a total population of 73,134.

The extraordinarily rapid progress of Catholicism in a country where chiefs and government officials were almost wholly in opposition, and where Protestant missionaries occupying high posts as advisers and counselors continued to oppose Catholicism, requires comment. There is no simple explanation, but it might be suggested that cultural and social pendulums were swinging back into a new equilibrium. That there was a tension among Hawaiians about the strictness of the new Protestantism is clear. The new Code of Laws of 1835, with its sanctions against fornication, divorce, and drunkenness, is only one example. Overall, the more tolerant attitude of the Catholics toward human frailties appealed to Hawaiians, and the grace of God dispensed through the tenderness of the Virgin and a host of forgiving saints contrasted sharply with the sternness of the Protestant Iehovah. Since the 1820s, periodic outbreaks of native revivalism, often combining

Christian thought adapted to ancient Hawaiian practices through various syncretistic formulas, gave further evidence that the religious needs of many Hawaiians were not being fulfilled by Protestant doctrine alone.

And finally, there was the undoubted connection made by many Hawaiians between the images of the Catholic pantheon and their vanished idols. The protestations of the enemies of the Catholics about the "idolatry" of the Romans may even have reinforced this connection in Hawaiian minds. As the regent Kinau is reported to have said by way of explaining her antipathy to Catholicism, she did not charge the Catholics themselves with idolatry, but rather felt that they "gathered persons disposed to idolatry, and that those persons were idolators, that is, they practiced Roman Catholic ceremonies with the same notions they had previously cherished."

Despite official toleration and rapid progress in conversion, however, many difficulties persisted for the Catholic mission. In effect, the Catholics at the beginning were in much the same position the Protestants had found themselves in two decades before. Everything was needed at once: money, materials, and additional priests and lay workers. In 1840 the mission had only a simple catechism and a spelling book printed that year in Honolulu for use in school work, and fewer than a dozen instructors were available.

The setting up and maintenance of a solid parochial school system was the principal concern of the Catholics, just as religious instruction had been the focus of the activity of their predecessors a generation before. Early in 1841 Father Maigret opened a teacher training school, which was flourishing within three years. In 1846 land was granted to the mission at Ahuimanu on the windward side of Oahu for a seminary similar to that directed by the Protestants at Lahainaluna. A second Catholic press was established in 1845, and from that time it supplied the schools and the seminary with the necessary printed materials.

The Catholic mission was able to support only a limited number of schools, however. Most children of that faith attended the so-called government "common schools," which, while officially nonsectarian, were in fact under the control of a Protestant-oriented school agency, at the head of which was a strongly anti-Catholic figure, David Malo. Catholic objections to what they regarded as limitations on their freedom to teach their religion mounted in the late 1840s, and there was a continuing concern that the Hawaiian authorities were basically hostile to the mission and that its survival depended on the ultimate threat of renewed French intervention.

The complaints of the Catholics were taken up and used as a political cudgel, as had so often been the case before, by the newly arrived French consul. Once again, in 1849, French warships arrived to present a series of demands; the most unacceptable to the Hawaiian authorities was the demand that government schools in which a majority of the pupils were Catholic (most common schools were sharply divided on a confessional basis, with a heavy majority of either Protestants or Catholics) be placed under the control of the Catholic mission. The Hawaiian government, whose position had been greatly strengthened in the preceding years by joint international recognition of its independence, rejected the demand, which was renewed in diluted form in 1851 only to be refused again. The problem was finally resolved when the minister of public instruction secularized all public schools in 1854, placing them on a strictly territorial rather than a sectarian basis. Many objections to this were raised by many parties—including the Mormon mission, which by then was actively proselytizing—but the system was gradually put into effect and proved to be workable. After 1860 educational confessionalism was no longer a serious problem.

By the time of the death of Kamehameha III in 1854, the Catholic mission was firmly established. As the official historian of the mission wrote at that time: "Persecution had passed forever, and none but the ordinary difficulties had to be coped with. . . ." And a few years later, in 1866, Mark Twain praised the leadership of Bishop Maigret in these words: "The French Roman Catholic Mission here, under the Right Reverend Lord Bishop Maigret, goes along quietly and unostentatiously; and its affairs are conducted with a wisdom which betrays the presence of a leader of distinguished ability. The Catholic clergy are honest, straight-forward, frank, and open; they are industrious and devoted to their religion and their work; they never meddle; whatever they do can be relied on as being prompted by a good and worthy motive."

By 1860 the Catholic press was publishing extensively, and in that year was begun a periodical publication that later came to be known as *Ka Hae Katholika* (The Catholic Standard). The year before, ten sisters of the Congregation of the Sacred Hearts had founded a school for girls next to the cathedral; the school still exists as the Academy of the

Sacred Hearts in the Kaimuki area of Honolulu. And in 1881 St. Louis College, the successor to the Ahuimanu high school, began dispensing Catholic higher education in Honolulu.

Although Bishop Maigret played the crucial role in leading the mission to a position of entrenched stability from which Catholicism could grow, as it has, to become the leading denomination in Hawaii today, to most of the world the outstanding figure in the history of the Catholic church in Hawaii is Joseph de Veuster, Father Damien. The celebrated Belgian priest, minister to the lepers, worked among the afflicted in the isolation area on the island of Molokai from 1873 until his death there from the disease in 1889.

Father Damien, born in Belgium, was one of many Flemish priests whose contributions to the spiritual and material history of Hawaii have been far in excess of their number. He was ordained in Honolulu and worked on the island of Hawaii before volunteering to go to Molokai. He was active at first in other areas of that island, and the charming country church of St. Joseph at Kamalo is testimony to his work and gentle spirit as much as is St. Philomena at the site of the leper colony on the isolated peninsula of Kalaupapa, where he served for many years. His body remained at the site of the colony until 1936, when it was returned to Belgium for reburial. His fame may be considered equal to that of the founder of the Hawaiian kingdom, Kamehameha the Great, for the state legislature of Hawaii chose these two historical figures to be honored by having their statues placed in the state's niche at the Capitol in Washington, D.C. A copy of the sculpture of Father Damien has also been placed in the atrium of the capitol building of the State of Hawaii in Honolulu.

*   *   *

For about a generation after 1840 the preponderant imprint on Hawaiian Catholicism remained French. But by the 1860s the faith was being given new impetus and diversity as Belgian priests from the Order of the Sacred Hearts appeared in increasing numbers and carried their labors and devotion to outlying districts. One of the outstanding representatives of this group, Father John (born Joseph Velghe in Belgium), was responsible for the beautiful painted church in Honaunau on the island of Hawaii, in which a *trompe-l'oeil* effect reproduces within the miniature wooden structure the glories of the Cathedral of Burgos in Spain and transmutes them into a tropical setting with translations of the scriptures into Hawaiian. A disciple of his, Father Evarist, also from Belgium, painted the ceiling of an equally beautiful country church, the Star of the Sea, at the black sand beach of Kalapana on the same island.

Even more important was the growth of Hawaiian membership in the church and its gradual transformation. This was much aided by the immigration of a large contingent of Portuguese from the Azores and Madeira as workers, beginning in 1878. By the turn of the century the Portuguese, who made up ten percent of the population, were established as a distinctive community in Hawaii, and they fortified the Catholic church not only by their presence but through extensive intermarriage with Hawaiians. Perhaps the most notable of their contributions is found on the slopes of Kula, on Maui, where a considerable number settled and built the octagonal church Our Lady Queen of Angels, with altar paintings and stations of the cross depicted on panels executed in the far-off Austrian Tyrol and transported to Hawaii.

There is little doubt that the definitive imprint left on Hawaiian culture was that shaped by the New England missionaries, and that Hawaii will never lose that anchor rock. But a rich and varied counterpoint was provided by the contributions of Catholic men and women from many nations in Europe and their dependencies in the islands of the Atlantic and the Pacific—from France and Belgium, Portugal and the Azores, Chile, and from the Philippines in most recent times—who all together have helped to link Hawaii to the mainstream of Latin Christianity and to enhance singularly the spiritual and material heritage of the islands.

The Gathering
of the Saints

THE STORY OF THE MORMON MOVEMENT in Hawaii is as much a chronicle of extremes and improbabilities as it is on the American continent. It has been well described as "one of the tallest of tall tales," and would be nearly unbelievable were it not for the clearly visible translation of a dream of history into the reality of today and the outline of tomorrow.

On the American mainland the Mormon saga is that of a persecuted sect, once treated as a virtual outlaw from the community, that passed from federal condemnation as an organized rebellion to staid respectability and ultimately to elite minority status in the modern world. This group founded its own kingdom in the deserts of the American West, shed the socially dubious virtues of polygamy in favor of a puritanical monogamy, then turned outward to spread its evangelistic gospel to the ends of the earth.

The history of the Mormons is one of faith, activism, and an unstaunchable will to prevail, qualities buttressed by the inner resilience given to a group that feels itself to be beleaguered and besieged. The strength of the Mormons came in part from the brightly shining quality of their vision, in part from the bitterness of the reaction to this vision by the early American tradition, which was founded on the separation of church and state and held in abhorrence the Mormon concept of a hierarchical community upholding a unique faith and functioning as a state within the state.

Because the community was persecuted it was, in a reciprocal cause-and-effect relationship, proselytizing—eager and indeed compelled to explain its claims to truth. And because it was beleaguered and isolated, it was driven to carry out policies of economy and austerity, and to foster among its followers qualities of self-reliance and mutual help that would ensure its survival under difficult and disadvantageous circumstances. Zealousness and sound—some even say sharp—economic practice have marked the movement since its inception.

The freedom to seek salvation, found in the open spaces of Utah, finally led the Mormons on to farther frontiers, to the gold fields of California and eventually across the Pacific to Hawaii and all Polynesia after 1850, the last areas open for new conquests of the spirit.

*   *   *

The Church of Jesus Christ of Latter-day Saints came into being, like many other home-grown religious bodies in the early nineteenth century on the American frontier, as a faith founded on new revelations and unique institutions. The revelations of its first president and prophet, Joseph Smith, were transmitted in the form of the tablets making up the Book of Mormon. These are complemented by the Bible, the Doctrine and Covenants, and the revelation known as the Pearl of Great Price, all of which are held to be the word of God. The institutions of the church combined lay participation—an important feature of all native American churches—with the highly structured ranking of officials headed by a president and two counselors, assisted by twelve apostles.

The church was founded in upper New York State in 1830, but its adherents soon moved west in search of greater religious freedom, first to Ohio, then to Missouri and Illinois. Wherever the Mormons settled, their doctrinal intransigence and their tight economic and social organization aroused hostility, and in 1844 Joseph Smith and his brother were fatally shot while being held in jail in Carthage, Illinois. This incident led the majority of Mormons to make the long trek westward beyond the Rocky Mountains to the lands of the Great Basin that are now Utah—uninhabited save by Indians, who were on the whole more hospitable than the white neighbors of the Mormons had been. There by the shores of the Great Salt Lake they founded their hermit state of Deseret in July 1847, and proceeded in time to construct their temple and tabernacle.

The splendid isolation of the new Zion lasted only a few years, until the gold rush to California made the area a way station on the road west. The gold fields also seemed to Mormon leaders a fertile field for teaching and conversion, and in keeping with the principle that all members of the church must do field service, they dispatched a missionary group to California. The mission was predictably a failure, and it was decided to send some of the missionaries on to the "Kingdom of the Sandwich Islands," which, it was hoped, would provide a more promising field for saving souls. The small group of ten set sail from San Francisco in November 1850, and after a voyage of three weeks arrived in Honolulu on December 12.

The Mormons expected to make converts among the white inhabitants of the islands, but there were few of those and their allegiance was already acquired. The most fruitful area was clearly among the natives, but this required language study, and to this the Mormon missionaries who remained turned their efforts. The mission workers had been divided two to an island, and the pair assigned to Maui included George Cannon, who proved to be adept in both language learning and organizational skills during the four years he worked there. The first Mormon church in Hawaii was built during his tenure there, and with the help of two local converts he began to translate the Book of Mormon into Hawaiian in January 1852. The work was completed two years later and printed in San Francisco.

The Mormons meanwhile experienced active hostility and opposition from the already established Protestant and Catholic functionaries, as well as from native chiefs who adhered to those faiths. But they persevered and gradually prospered. According to the official census, by 1853 they already numbered 2,778, and in that and the following year there was steady growth. At first the only Mormon schools were for the purpose of teaching English, but by the end of 1853 the Mormon community was asking for separate common schools supported by the government on a basis of equality with their Protestant and Catholic counterparts.

The success of the Mormons in the first years of their mission is not hard to understand. For one thing, their operations were quite different from those of other religious missions. Missionaries were young, poor, and usually amiable and unostentatious, living simply and in close contact with the Hawaiians. They served only a few years and were rotated regularly, so that their positions did not become privileged sinecures. Moreover, they quickly began to appoint Hawaiians to official positions within the church, something that was facilitated both by the structural organization of the Latter-day Saints, in which a hierarchical niche was available for many, and by the fact that Hawaiians were by midcentury much more educated and consequently more capable of serving in ecclesiastical offices.

Mormon success is explicable at another level as well. The Latter-day Saints were an exotic band of Christians who had the appeal of the new and the different to many Hawaiians. They set themselves apart from both Catholic and Protestant and proclaimed that they were the "restored" church of Jesus Christ. To their newly converted Hawaiian flock they offered an intensely personal vision of salvation and a chance, indeed an obligation, to work for it in concert with their brethren. The sense of brotherhood and closeness instilled by the minority position in which the Mormons found themselves in Hawaii clearly appealed to the ancient communal feelings of Hawaiians, to their cooperative sense of *laulima*, the Hawaiian feeling of togetherness. The New England pastors and the Catholic priests had brought alien concepts of the godhead that prevailed to the degree that Hawaiian confidence in their own culture had disintegrated, and the relationship the outsiders had established with the natives was inherently an unequal one of giver and receiver, teacher and pupil. The Mormons, on the other hand, almost immediately offered full participation in a common endeavor, in which all were saints and all were seeking refuge and strength through sharing the burden of their faith. And finally, the Mormons brought identity in the form of a charismatic community, with a message that anyone who joined them would be a member of a very special group, apart from and superior to all others. This amalgam of exclusivity and moral superiority had a great attraction for Hawaiians in the midstream of change in which they were foundering in the 1850s.

Just at this time, the Mormon elders who had founded their new state in the American West were thinking in terms of gathering in all converts of the Latter-day Saints to the Utah homeland. The Saints were held to be always potentially subject to persecution for their convictions; their physical safety and their moral salvation could only be assured in a defensible and righteous community where they would be safe from both oppression and temptation.

In the interim, timely refuges might be arranged if necessary. Mormon elders in Hawaii were of course aware of these plans for an eventual gathering of the Saints, and they felt that the Hawaiian community needed a temporary shelter in view of the bitter verbal and physical attacks so often made on them. In 1853 they wrote for advice on this matter to President Brigham Young, who recommended their establishing an independent community of their own: "In the meantime, I will suggest that if possible you obtain a fitting island or part of an island where the brethren can collect in peace and sustain themselves unmolested, it might be much pleasanter for them, and they be better able to prepare themselves for gathering to this continent when the way shall open."

Providence soon provided. Shortly after this exchange of correspondence, a Mormon leader visited the small island of Lanai, a few miles in the lee of Maui, where mission work had been so successful, and described it as an ideal site for setting up a colony of Saints. The island was largely uninhabited and most of it was owned by a high chief, Haalelea, who generously gave the free use of it to the Mormon community for four years, after which it might be purchased. On July 26, 1854, the decision was formally taken to "gather the Saints" on the island of Lanai, and a group of elders headed by Joseph F. Smith, later the sixth president of the church, was charged with the task. There, in the interior of the barren, brush-strewn island, a site was selected and named the City of Joseph. By the close of 1854, which marked the end of the reign of Kamehameha III, streets had been laid out, houses were being built, land was under cultivation, and the Saints seemed to have planted firm roots in the soil of Lanai.

*   *   *

But this was not to be the case. For the next decade the Latter-day Saints underwent a series of tribulations and setbacks in their Lanai settlement that almost caused the community to come apart. The first blow was the withdrawal of the American elders from the scene in 1858, upon instructions from President Brigham Young. The recall orders were due partly to reports reaching Utah indicating a certain disarray in the mission, and partly to the internal difficulties of the Mormon community during its so-called civil war in Utah.

Upon their departure, the American leaders appointed Hawaiians to head the mission and care for the Lanai gathering. The Hawaiians were in the end unequal to the task, and as the official history of the mission notes: ". . . the native Elders continued to preach and baptize as they had been in the habit of doing before the American elders left, but a spirit of carelessness and indifference soon became prevalent in many of the branches. . . . Many members drifted back to old habits."

Clearly the time had not come, either for the Mormons or other denominations in which licensing and ordination of native converts was increasing, when leadership could be left entirely in local hands. And other difficulties arose when the community was unable to raise money to purchase the land on which the City of Joseph was located.

At this juncture, providence appeared to bestow a boon once again in the arrival on the scene of a rare and adventurous soul whose personality was to mark the history of the Hawaiian kingdom for more than a quarter of a century. This was Walter Murray Gibson, who was schoolteacher, merchant, author, rogue, religious leader, and high public official in the course of a remarkably varied life lived to the full.

After a youthful period of involvement with political intrigue in lands as distant as Guatemala and the East Indies, Gibson returned to the United States and became attracted to the Mormon community, which he visited in Salt Lake City in 1859. He proposed to church authorities the establishment of a Mormon state somewhere in the Pacific, an idea that eventually bore unexpected fruit. Brigham Young remained skeptical, but when Gibson gave seeming evidence of the sincerity of his interest in Mormonism by receiving baptism in 1860, the church gave him a general commission as a missionary in the Pacific.

Armed with this document, which assured his acceptance by the now demoralized Hawaiian community on Lanai, Gibson arrived in Honolulu on July 4, 1861. Within a short period he restructured the Mormon organization along the lines of the mother church in Utah, with himself as "Chief President of the Islands of the Sea and the Hawaiian Islands," aided by ordained apostles, priests, and bishops. His entrepreneurial skills and oratorical ability together revived the flagging community in regard to both membership and financial stability. With money from induced collections and the sale of church offices for handsome fees, he gathered enough funds to buy the lands occupied by the Saints on Lanai, replenished them with livestock, and planted crops anew. The City of Joseph was given a second chance to flourish and grow.

But Gibson had stacked the cards against himself and thus against a tranquil future for the community. At times he seemed to be genuinely devoted to the life of the Saints on Lanai; at other times the call to adventure led him to rail against the intellectual and physical barrenness of existence on the tiny island. And he became suspect in the eyes of many of the brethren because of his lack of knowledge of church practice. Some of the disaffected among the Hawaiians accordingly wrote to Mormon headquarters in Utah and an investigatory delegation of two apostles and three elders was dispatched to the scene in the spring of 1864.

The Board of Inquiry found evidence of wayward practices, corruption, and personal aggrandizement sufficient to cause them to excommunicate Gibson, who, among other things, had recorded the deeds on the Lanai lands in his own name. The faithful were allowed to choose between leaving Lanai for another site where the church would be organized again, or remaining in apostasy with their deposed leader, who refused to surrender his illegally gotten properties. Most of the Saints remained within the fold and the mission was reorganized by two American elders sent from Utah, George Nebeker and Francis Hammond. They decided to relocate the community in a secluded site on the windward side of Oahu, on six thousand acres stretching from the mountains to the sea, about a fourth of which was suitable for farming. The gathering at Laie, like the Lanai settlement, was intended to be self-sufficient; it was a plantation as well as a town site, and church members contributed as field workers while also serving as lay brethren.

This practice aroused criticism from outsiders, who charged that Hawaiians were being exploited by the mission for its financial gain. But King Kalakaua years later refused to sign a draft law forbidding such employment unless it dealt with working conditions for all employees of all churches, and the issue died. Although conditions were often grim because of natural disasters like drought and flooding, and despite the fluctuation of wages—often paid in scrip and redeemable only within the settlement—the plantation and the community eventually flourished. Subsidies arrived from Utah, the local leadership was honest, and the Hawaiian members of the gathering were firm in their dedication. Gradually improvements were made; a power mill was built, artesian wells were drilled, and later a pumping system was installed. Although rice, tobacco, and coffee were intermittently grown, sugar cane was the main crop, and it sustained the mission from the beginnings until it was leased to a commercial plantation in 1931. The Saints, left in peace and guided by conscientious stewardship, gradually increased their prosperity and their numbers. According to official church records, membership by 1879 amounted to 4,408 people, about one-tenth of the Hawaiian population of the islands.

*　　　*　　　*

Just after World War I ended, the Mormon dream of constructing a temple in Hawaii became a reality. On November 27, 1919, the grandiose edifice set in a formal garden flanked by long rows of trees was dedicated by President Heber Grant in Laie, a fitting ceremony for that Thanksgiving Day. In succeeding years the Mormon community emerged from its near seclusion and spread to other parts of Oahu and then to other islands, a trend that was accentuated when the plantation was leased in 1931. After World War II the Latter-day Saints embarked on a vigorous program of expanding their activities, and by 1954 there were nine thousand church members in the Oahu Stake alone.

It had long been part of the Mormon vision to complement the temple at Laie with an institution of higher learning that would serve as a beacon throughout the Pacific, and this project also formed part of the steady postwar growth of the community. Plans were laid as early as 1947, and eight years later ground was broken for Church College. The college opened in September 1955 mostly with temporary buildings, and was completed in 1958 with the help of an extraordinary volunteer labor mission that contributed almost 300,000 man-hours to its construction. In 1974 it was renamed Brigham Young University—Hawaii.

The temple and college at Laie were in and for Hawaii to be sure, but they were also institutions meant for all Pacific islanders. Since the mid-nineteenth century the Latter-day Saints had sent missions throughout Polynesia—to Tonga, Samoa, the Cook Islands, and elsewhere—and established firm footholds in the South Pacific. In part the reason for their success lay in the same kind of devotion and meticulous organization that they had shown in Hawaii, but in larger measure it reflected the unique place given to Polynesians in Mormon cosmology.

The Book of Mormon, which is accepted as gospel by the Mormon church, holds that a band of Israelites fled the destruction of the kingdom of Israel and captivity in Babylon and went to America to found its own state. Eventually war broke out between two of the groups, and one of them, the Nephites, including Mormon himself, was completely destroyed, although Moroni, the son of Mormon, survived to hide the golden tablets for later revelation to the prophet Joseph Smith. It was also held, however, that a branch of the Nephites was preserved in the Pacific, to become the Polynesians—who, as part of one of the lost tribes, are thus direct descendants of the Israelites.

Fanciful as this tale may seem, the skillful use of the story to reinforce the Polynesian custom of chanting the genealogy of a family back to the distant past had great appeal for many Pacific islanders. The individual and his family were thus linked to the Mormon faith and given an identity in antiquity consonant with their new religious beliefs. Ancestry and lineage took on new stature and their prestige was enhanced; the chants were no longer a parochial and heathen recital of the past but now became part of a universal manifestation of God's will to preserve his chosen people through the vicissitudes of history. And the Polynesians could believe themselves truly chosen through their revealed wanderings from Jerusalem to Aotearoa, the Land of the Long White Cloud at the other end of the earth. A journey of two thousand years thus ended with redemption from the endless pagan past. Who indeed can claim that they have not been chosen?

5

Church and State: Anglican Hawaii

Today we begin a new era. Let it be one of increased civilization, one of decided progress, in-
dustry, temperance, morality, and all of those
virtues which mark a nation's advance.
          —Inauguration speech of Kamehameha IV
                                       January 11, 1855

SHORTLY AFTER 1860 THE FLEDGLING Hawaiian kingdom began to
sketch in the outlines of a new and more mature character. Its capital,
now fixed in Honolulu, blossomed forth with a first burst of cosmopol-
itanism. Although the town was still a drab and dusty South Seas port
along its waterfront, the mountains and valleys behind the city held
increasing numbers of solid, stately homes and summer retreats. Their
broad *lanais*, or verandas, their shade trees, and the close-cropped lawns

that surrounded them reflected the gracefully indolent life led by the court, the native aristocracy, and the *kamaaina* families of missionaries and merchants now solidly established and entwined in the affairs of state. All these groups were increasingly interlinked through intermarriage between people of chiefly lineage and native landowners on the one hand and the recently arrived merchants and traders on the other. And so there was brought into being an expanding body of mixed bloods who were not only accepted into local society but who eventually emerged as the dominant element in it, giving it finally a style and a distinction that it had hitherto lacked, and which became during the following two or three decades the basis of much that is quintessentially Hawaiian to this day.

The spirit of this Hawaiian springtime—romantic, hopeful, naive, somewhat pretentious, but always with a self-knowing current of *opéra bouffe* running through it in a way that must have made it as delicious to live through as it is delectable to conjure up a century later—was symbolized by the accession to the throne in 1854 of the fourth Kamehameha, Alexander Liholiho—a stylish, bright, and elegant youth who had been well educated at the Chiefs' School and who later had traveled to Europe and America in the company of Finance Minister and Special Emissary Judd in 1849–50. Two years after his accession, in 1856, Alexander Liholiho married his childhood sweetheart, Emma Rooke, in a ceremony at Kawaiahao presided over by the Reverend Richard Armstrong and jubilantly acclaimed by the Hawaiian people.

Emma's grace and charm set their mark on the succeeding epoch as much as did the qualities of her husband, and her background epitomized the changing nature of Hawaii: the granddaughter of Keliimaikai, younger brother of Kamehameha the Great, on her father's side, and through her mother the granddaughter of John Young, the English adviser to that king when he was still a high chief of the island of Hawaii. The new queen was the first reigning consort of mixed blood and had been raised by her foster father, Dr. T. C. B. Rooke, an English physician long resident in Hawaii. Her education at the Chiefs' School and by private tutors had imbued her with a lively attitude and an inquiring mind. This blended well with her English upbringing at Rooke House, one of the first of the *haole*-type homes in the town, which, with their upper-story wraparound balconies and wooden Corinthian columns, today call to mind the antebellum country houses of the Old South.

The tastes of the aristocratic and sometimes impetuous young king were equally cosmopolitan. Reared by sermonizing and exhortation by the American Mission, he felt an antipathy to all things missionary, as his mentor, Dr. Judd, once admitted. And he was impressed by the English style of life as he experienced it during his visit to England as an adolescent with his brother Lot, who was later to become Kamehameha V. His marriage to Emma Rooke, who was widely believed to be his childhood sweetheart, felicitously allowed each member of the royal couple to reinforce the pro-English sentiments of the other.

But other, more political factors were working to create a climate of sympathy toward English ways in Hawaii in the 1850s. In the preceding decade the French had been the main threat to Hawaiian independence, but after the discovery of gold in California and the entry of that state into the Union in 1850, America had suddenly become the nearest neighbor to Hawaii—a power whose closeness to and growingly preponderant interest in the mid-Pacific kingdom seemed to many Hawaiians to represent a new kind of danger.

As San Francisco rapidly became a major port, ocean transport began to forge the first links in a chain that would eventually bind the Hawaiian Islands firmly to mainland America. Packet boats from California started to serve the islands shortly after 1850, and a regular shipping service was inaugurated in 1867. And as the commercial predominance of the United States grew, so did the political ambitions of adventurers in California looking for facile conquests, and of some American residents in Hawaii as well. In 1852, a congressman from the new state in the Golden West openly called for annexation of the kingdom by the United States. And in 1853, in the waning days of the reign of Kamehameha III, a self-styled "Committee of Thirteen" had forced the resignation of Dr. Judd and threatened to overthrow the monarchy with the help of "volunteers" from the West Coast. Finally, as the king lay ill in 1854, he was persuaded to ask the United States to consider establishing some kind of special relationship with Hawaii: both a reciprocity treaty and outright annexation were discussed, and at the death of Kamehameha III only his signature was required to make the latter a reality.

Thus, when the young Alexander Liholiho ascended the throne at the end of 1854, foreign policy, domestic policy, and religious affairs were converging in the direction of an effort to redress what the Hawaiian government perceived as the perilous situation of the state by adopting a more pro-British stance. One of the first acts of the new king was to make clear his determination to end any further discussion of annexation by America and to substitute for it a conjoint guarantee of Hawaiian independence by the principal sea powers, the United States, Britain, and France, a policy that—although it eventually came to naught—may well have helped to dissuade some of the more hot-headed American schemers and filibusterers from intemperate acts against the sovereignty of the kingdom, or at least to postpone them for several decades. In this climate the proposed Reciprocity Treaty failed to materialize, and, denied the burgeoning markets of California and Oregon, the economic health of Hawaii remained unstable and gradually developed more serious complications as the years passed.

Perhaps the final straw in the Hawaiian assessment of American intentions concerned the unforeseeable consequences of the struggle that divided the United States beginning in 1861. New foreign policy judgments had to be made when the Civil War broke out and America showed itself to be bitterly split, with California claiming adherents of both causes and being considered a prize by both sides. In the first two years of the conflict, which coincided with the last years of the reign of Kamehameha IV, British sympathies for the Confederacy and the high-handed impunity with which the Royal Navy behaved toward the Union government made their mark in Hawaiian minds. In August 1861 the Hawaiian government issued a proclamation of neutrality toward the parties to the conflict; but the chief minister to the king felt that the Confederacy would win its independence and should be accorded belligerent rights. Viewed through the prism of American violence and unpredictability, an impartial English presence and presiding power seemed possibly more attractive than ever to the Hawaiians.

During this period, moreover, a series of personal happenings contributed to the climate favoring the establishment of an Anglican church in Hawaii. In May 1858 the royal consort gave birth to a son, and the happy event gave rise to joyous celebrations throughout the land. For the first time in Hawaiian history the colorful style of a happy royal family took root in the public heart. The heir to the throne was significantly christened with an Anglo-Hawaiian name—Albert Edward Kauikeaouli Leiopapa o Kamehameha—and was called, in the European manner, the Prince of Hawaii.

A year later the foreign minister, Dr. Robert Crichton Wyllie, was taken gravely ill at his home, Rosebank, in the Nuuanu Valley. Wyllie was a Scotsman who had come to Hawaii in 1843 en route home from Mexico but who remained for twenty-two years, first serving as British proconsul in Honolulu, and then from 1845 until his death twenty years later as the faithful representative of his adopted country in the post of Minister of Foreign Affairs. Like so many other foreigners who helped fashion the saga of Hawaii, he came for a brief stopover of a few weeks and never left the islands, contributing much to the changing course of their history. After his convalescence ended at Washington Place, later the residence of Liliuokalani, the last queen of Hawaii, and now the official home of the governor of the state, he returned home with a renewed feeling for the comfort afforded by religion.

An even more unfortunate occurrence had meanwhile led the young king to much the same conclusion. The impetuous nature of Alexander Liholiho's character came to the surface at the same time in a banal incident in which the king, made violently jealous because of false reports about a liaison between his American secretary and the queen, shot and seriously wounded his personal adviser. Alexander Liholiho was overcome by contrition after the deed and sought ways to make amends. His self-reproach at one time was so great that it led him to consider abdicating in favor of his infant son, but he was finally dissuaded from such a step. He became more aware of the consoling virtues of religion, however, and he returned to his earlier idea of building an Episcopal church in his kingdom with the help of the British, whose formal and monarchical ways he so much admired.

It was the strange convergence of all these strands of fate that ultimately led to a letter from Wyllie to Manley Hopkins, the Hawaiian consul general in London, in December 1859, asking him to make inquiries for a proper Anglican clergyman who would be willing to come to Hawaii. The king proposed to give land for a church and to pay the salary and lodgings of the new priest. It was stressed that this was a private, not an official offer, for the firm beliefs of the early American missionaries about the separation of church and state had been enshrined in the Hawaiian constitution and firmly inculcated into Hawaiian thinking.

In London, Hopkins undertook his charge with zeal. He organized a Committee for Promoting the English Church in Polynesia, and wrote an amateur work of history, *The Past, Present and Future of the Kingdom of Hawaii*. This was published in 1862 with a preface by the Bishop of Oxford, Samuel Wilberforce, who turned out to be the prime mover within the British establishment in favor of the church project. And soon, as all such plans do, this one grew almost out of recognition—from the first concept of a simple chapel and clergyman to the more ambitious idea of a highly organized missionary bishopric in the Pacific. The Bishop of Oxford was in good part responsible for championing the enlarged plan, and after it had been approved in England its advantages were suggested to Kamehameha IV, who readily understood them and gave his approval.

The extended scope of the project required more money and time, and an appeal for help was made to Queen Victoria from the Hawaiian throne. No direct answer was received, but Secretary of State for Foreign Affairs Lord Russell in his reply wrote of the "great satisfaction" of the queen, while pointing out that she had no way to give personal or official assistance in such matters to foreign countries, which could only count on what was voluntarily contributed by British subjects. At the same time, Wyllie informed the Archbishop of Canterbury of the project and asked for his approval as primate of the Church of England. Again there was seemingly no direct answer, but in the following spring of 1861, a convocation of high officials of the Church of England discussed the matter with what appears to have been a favorable bias.

In August of that year, the Archbishop of Canterbury gave his full approval by designating the Reverend Thomas Nettleton Staley, of Queen's College, Cambridge, as bishop of the Hawaiian diocese. After some debate as to the need for royal sanction, it was agreed that a license from Queen Victoria would be necessary, and this was given on December 15, 1861, at which time the Reverend Mr. Staley was formally consecrated in his post as Bishop of the Church of England in Hawaii.

After many delays, Bishop Staley and his family sailed from England in August 1862 and were expected in Honolulu within two months. The arrival of the bishop was awaited with eagerness and excitement, for he had a special role to play in the emerging church-state tie that was being forged by Alexander Liholiho and Emma. The bishop was to serve as preceptor to the young Prince of Hawaii, now four years old, and the first ceremonial act of the prelate was to be the baptism of the heir to the throne. The ceremonial importance of this act was underlined by the fact that Queen Victoria had agreed to be godmother to the Prince of Hawaii—who was part English by blood—and was presenting a silver cup to her godson on the occasion.

The cup was carried to Honolulu by the new British consul general, William Synge, who was scheduled to arrive shortly before Staley. On his disembarkation he received the sad news that the young prince lay desperately ill. Acting with generosity and statesmanship in response to a request from the royal parents, Consul Synge agreed to act as proxy for the Prince of Wales as godfather to the dying child, and a baptismal ceremony was held *in extremis* under moving circumstances, only a few days before the prince died on August 27, 1862.

Bishop Staley and his retinue arrived early in October while the king and queen were away from Honolulu. After they returned, the official sermon that formally inaugurated the Episcopal mission was delivered by the bishop in the royal presence. Shortly thereafter Queen Emma was baptized, and she and Kamehameha IV were confirmed as members of what was officially designated the Hawaiian Reformed Catholic Church. They were followed by a number of ministers, including Wyllie himself; the king's father Matthew Kekuanaoa, Governor of Oahu; and High Chief (later King) David Kalakaua. The new church had clearly attracted prestigious patronage at its very inception, even though some of the *ali'i* who were later to rule the kingdom, such as King Lunalilo (reigned 1873–74) and Queen Liliuokalani (reigned 1891–93), remained faithful to Kawaiahao.

The enthusiasm of Alexander and Emma sustained the church in its initial months. The king had already translated the Book of Common Prayer into Hawaiian, and in November of 1862 the Morning Prayer service was held in Hawaiian for the first time. In the preface to the translated volume, Kamehameha IV harked back to one of the first English benefactors of the kingdom: "The Church is established here in Hawaii through the breathings of the Holy Spirit and by the agency of the chiefs. Vancouver, years ago, was requested to send us the True God."

The land promised for the cathedral, to be called after St. Peter, was duly provided. St. Alban's School for Boys was established, and plans were laid for the first church on Maui. Bishop Staley and the Episcopal Mission were deeply interested in education for young women, and by 1868 nine boarding schools had been founded, with an attendance of some three hundred Hawaiian girls.

Late in 1863, however, the Anglican cause received a serious blow when Alexander Liholiho died. The health of the king, who was only twenty-nine years of age, had always been delicate, and after the death of his only son he and the queen had retired to a country house outside Honolulu, where they led a life of quietude that contrasted sharply with the king's more exuberant earlier days. His brother and successor to the throne, Prince Lot Kamehameha, had considerably less interest in defending the new faith—he was said to have encouraged the resurrection of ancient Hawaiian rites and dances—and so the burden of supporting the church fell on the widowed Queen Emma.

Kamehameha IV died on November 30, Saint Andrew's Day, so the name of the cathedral that was being planned was changed to St. Andrew's, while St. Alban's School was given the poetic name of Iolani (Bird of Heaven). A procathedral was built in 1866 on the site of the land given by the late king, *mauka* (inland) of the royal palace, where the present St. Andrew's Cathedral now stands. The Dowager Queen Emma traveled to England on behalf of the cathedral and obtained architectural advice as well as contributions for its construction. The cornerstone was laid in March 1867 and work began, but at a slow pace.

Priority was given, in accordance with Bishop Staley's views, to building a school for girls to be known as St. Andrew's Priory. While in England Queen Emma had the good fortune to meet Miss Sellon, the mother superior of the Sisters of the Holy Trinity, who enthusiastically supported the idea of sending women teachers out to Hawaii, and who, in answer to a later entreaty by the bishop and the queen, came herself to the islands in 1867, oversaw the building of the priory, and was present at its dedication that same year.

The later history of the Reformed Catholic Church in Hawaii is one of a struggle against the already established Christian denominations and of dissension within its own ranks. The high church Anglo-Catholicism affected by Bishop Staley and his successor alienated them from the American Protestants, who had suspicions about the political role of the Anglicans as well; and the Episcopalians were condemned by the Roman Catholics as separatists from the true faith. After journeys to England and America in quest of financial and personnel assistance, Bishop Staley returned somewhat disillusioned and resigned in 1870. His departure led to fears among the Hawaiian elite that the work of the bishopric would be turned over to the Americans, and an offer was indeed made to an American bishop by the authorities in England, but it was declined.

The vacant office was finally taken up by another English clergyman, the Reverend Alfred Willis, who arrived in Honolulu in 1872. Bishop Willis occupied his post for thirty years, until long after Hawaii had lost its independence. He preferred to call the church Anglican, although he continued to use a high church ritual that led a number of members of the congregation to form a schismatic second congregation. The bishop reworked the grandiose plans for St. Andrew's, and prepared to build it section by section. On Christmas Day in 1886 he held services in the parts that were completed—the present choir and first bay—and he lived to see the completion of two more bays in 1902.

More than anything, however, Bishop Willis was a royalist by conviction, and he proved to be a mainstay of the Hawaiian monarchy in its last beleaguered years. His support of Queen Liliuokalani with respect, among other matters, to her allowing the legalization of the sale of opium in 1892 left him almost alone in opposition to her own advisers, her pastor at Kawaiahao, and many of the Anglo-American businessmen who had broken with his brand of Anglicism. Strongly opposed to the American annexation of 1898 and discouraged by the difficulties he was meeting on all sides, Bishop Willis finally agreed that Episcopal work in Hawaii should be given over to the American branch of the church; and having presided over the consecration of St. Andrew's and seen its construction further advanced, he left the Hawaiian scene and undertook missionary work in Tonga during his last years.

*   *   *

It is difficult to assess the permanent influence of the Anglican church in Hawaii. Seen in one light, it was an incident that reflected the vagaries of the background and upbringing of both Alexander Liholiho and Emma, harmonized with the aristocratic nature of their personalities, and combined these fortuities with a shrewd political strategy.

That there was such a political motivation—from the Hawaiian side but not the British—is shown in much of the correspondence of the time, and notably in a letter from Kamehameha V to the widowed Queen Emma in 1871, in which he notes: "You and I perfectly feel the same, there was from the beginning a very great political reason, why the Mission from England should have had the support of all people who really loved their Country. It was never mooted by any one. We thought, get England to be interested in *us* by means of her Church, and let the Englishmen contribute their wealth Clergymen & laymen to ornament and sustain this Church, she will begin to learn more of us and take more interest in us. . . ."

Possibly this strategy was more successful than we shall ever know, and it may well have enabled the feeble kingdom to pass through the turbulent years of American history just before and during the Civil War. In the end, of course, the steadily growing power of America in the Pacific and the silken cords of the Reciprocity Treaty, which was finally signed in 1876, made inevitable the final steps of revolt by *haole* businessmen and their henchmen in 1893 and ultimate annexation at the time of the campaign for the Philippines in the Spanish-American war of 1898. Thus the "Anglican affair" at best only postponed what many Hawaiians had long foreseen as the unavoidable evil day.

But the association of the court with the Church of England had other less political consequences. It gave a new status of pious nobility to the royal family, and it helped create a style which, if sometimes it seemed too much that of the upstart emulating the crown of a global empire, still had its grace and dignity. The afterglow of that short period can best be seen today in the heirlooms and mementos found in Queen Emma's summer palace, Hanaiakalama, in the Nuuanu Valley above Honolulu, which is preserved as a museum, and in the hushed silence of the nearby Royal Mausoleum, built in the English manner in 1865 to house the remains of the kings and high chiefs of Hawaii.

All in all, though, the Anglican church let down no deep roots in Hawaiian society and life. It made little mark on later rulers as they became inescapably entangled with the American colossus, and even less on the Hawaiian commoners, who, representing less than half the total population by 1890, were being outpaced by white entrepreneurs and financiers and outstripped by the new immigrant laborers from the Orient who worshiped other gods.

Anglican Hawaii could be described in sum as a fleeting moment of might-have-been. If Kamehameha IV had lived even a few years more and had been able to nurture the embryonic movement to a point where he came to be looked upon by his people as the legitimate head of both their state and their church, indissolubly and without question joined together, then perhaps the subsequent history of Hawaii might have taken a quite different path.

6

Gifts from the Orient

DURING THE 1860S THE AMOUNT OF LAND given over to sugar plantations in Hawaii increased tenfold, at the same time that the native Hawaiian population was continuing a decline that had begun soon after the discovery of the islands by Cook in 1778. From a figure estimated at a quarter of a million at that time, the population had dwindled by 1872 to less than fifty thousand. The Hawaiians were not averse to working in the cane fields—as has often been claimed—but there were simply not enough of them, so other sources of labor had to be sought from abroad. With the arrival of these newcomers the making of modern Hawaii got under way, as economic growth paved the way for dramatic ethnic and cultural changes in the closing decades of the nineteenth century.

At first, consideration was given to bringing workers from lands with similar tropical climes: the other Polynesian islands, India and the East Indies, the sugar-growing island of Mauritius, and the lush Azores. The Chinese, a small number of whom had already entered Hawaii as coolies by 1860, and about whose conduct in Honolulu complaints were rife, were not thought to be all that desirable at the beginning; and Japan was still a closed country. There were difficulties on all sides; the Polynesians were few, the Indians unforthcoming, and the Portuguese expensive. In the end, it was admitted that the Chinese were close at hand, available, and cheap. So in 1865 two ships landed with some five hundred Chinese contract workers who formed the vanguard of a stream of arrivals from the Far East over the ensuing three decades. The Chinese were joined in 1868 by the first contingent of Japanese laborers, but Japanese immigration did not begin in earnest until around 1890. Nevertheless, by 1900 more than 25,000 Chinese and 61,000 Japanese had settled in Hawaii. Together they then made up the majority of the population of the newly formed territory, and they were on the way to changing the character of the islands permanently. Toward the close of the nineteenth century Hawaii was a South Seas kingdom in dissolution, changing into a self-styled republic and then an American territory, governed by a white oligarchy and made to function by the labor of Orientals.

If economic avarice was the spur to the immigration of Asians and their culture, the evil that maintained it was the contract labor system. This form of temporary near-slavery had been legalized in an act of 1850 treating labor relations, and under its provisions—which governed most Hawaiian and all foreign workers on the plantations—laborers could be returned for enforced service if they left their work, and they could be imprisoned at hard labor if they refused to continue working. Contracts might be made, and usually were with the Chinese, for five years; with other foreign groups they were normally of shorter duration. The munificent wages paid to the first Chinese contract laborers were four dollars a month, food, lodging, and a bonus of two dollars at Chinese New Year.

The manifest advantages of the system to the economic rulers of the islands—who indeed looked on Hawaii as one large plantation controlled by them—had to be balanced against the disrepute into which it had brought them. Especially after the American Civil War had ended and the abolition of slavery become a reality, opinion in the United States, Britain, and elsewhere condemned the Hawaiian state for its practice of forced servitude. And at home as well, voices were raised in the press and among the clergy calling for the dismantling of the system. Even in the legislature the subject was bitterly debated for several decades, but always in the end the interests of the plantation owners won out. A modified form of contract labor survived the end of the monarchy and—curiously reinforced by the American laws on the exclusion of the Chinese, which were extended to Hawaii after annexation—lasted well into the twentieth century.

Even the staunchest supporters of the system, however, were concerned by its basic instability. For one thing, it was held that the excess of men over women meant that many of the newcomers were not likely to be permanent settlers. But it ultimately led to a good deal of race mixture, as the Chinese often married Hawaiian women. Moreover, the propensity of the Chinese who had finished their work contracts to move into town and establish themselves as shopkeepers, skilled craftsmen, truck farmers, cooks, and laundrymen alarmed the white community as a whole and middle-class *haole* tradesmen in particular. Thus the theme of the "Chinese peril" dominated economic and political life in Hawaii in the closing decades of the century, leading eventually to the anti-Asiatic movement and to ever more restrictive legislation on the entry of Chinese workers. This culminated in 1892 in the Act Restricting Chinese Immigration, under the terms of which no Chinese could enter Hawaii unless he agreed to "engage in no trading or mechanical occupation other than domestic service or agricultural labor in the field or in sugar and rice mills."

It was the twin problems of the insatiable need for labor and the seeming insolubility of the Chinese question that led Hawaiian entrepreneurs in the 1880s to turn to Japan for labor. Prejudices against the Chinese did not at that time extend to the Japanese—in fact they did not appear until Japan showed itself to be a major Pacific power after the Russo-Japanese War of 1904–5. In the eighties, partly as the result of King Kalakaua's visit to Japan in 1881 and his friendly reception there, Japan was quite favorably viewed in Hawaiian circles. In the imperfect state of ethnological knowledge at that time the Japanese were considered a "cognate race" to the Hawaiians, and they were widely held to be a sober and industrious people who would contribute much to Hawaiian growth and development, as they ultimately did to a far greater extent than anyone at the time could have imagined.

It took several years of negotiations before the Japanese government agreed to allow a limited amount of emigration by its subjects to

Hawaii, but the details were finally completed and in February 1885 the first shipload of nearly a thousand Japanese men, women, and children arrived in Honolulu on the City of Tokio, characteristically, with a foreign service officer who was to serve as an inspector of Japanese immigrants aboard. In later years the Japanese government often proved to be a zealous overseer of the interests of its emigrants, and on occasion threatened to stop emigration because of unsatisfactory processing and working conditions.

Yet, despite vicissitudes of all kinds, the Japanese flourished in Hawaii as in no other foreign land, and the first trickle of immigrants soon became a flood. By 1924, when they were definitively excluded from further entry, more than 180,000 had come to the islands. Although many of these returned to Japan, a nucleus of permanent residents—and ultimately citizens—was formed, representing 40 percent of the entire population of Hawaii in 1910. Just before World War II the Japanese community numbered roughly 150,000 people, one-third of all the inhabitants of the territory, and today the Japanese make up the second largest ethnic group in the fiftieth state.

Surrounded on all sides by different lifeways and the alien customs of a Christian country, the Japanese carefully nurtured the cultural baggage they had brought with them. Like Aeneas, they carried their household gods to foreign shores and venerated them. They built in the Japanese style, better suited to Hawaii's tropical climate than to the harsh winters of the homeland: Buddhist temples and Shinto shrines, tea houses and communal baths, and whenever possible miniature Japanese gardens.

As the early American missionaries had done, the Japanese put great emphasis on education. They, too, founded schools and often attached them to their temples and shrines, in the manner of the temple schools that had flourished in nineteenth-century Tokugawa Japan before the Meiji Restoration of 1868 and the advent of universal education. But the mission of these schools was different from that of their earlier Christian counterparts. They were not intended to convert the natives or to educate them; on the contrary, they were designed to help the younger Japanese preserve their heritage, and it was the language, the customs, and the arts of the motherland that were taught. Thus, eventually, the exclusivity of the community, its size, and the paternal solicitude that it enjoyed from the authorities in Japan, as well as the success that frugality and hard-working habits produced, combined to bring down on the heads of the Japanese the hostility and suspicion of their neighbors, especially as Japanese-American relations worsened in the years and months immediately prior to the Pearl Harbor attack.

In 1934, more than 41,000 Japanese children attended the language schools, but after the outbreak of war in 1941 all the schools were closed, and many were given to charitable or public agencies like the Red Cross and the YMCA in a moment of panic on the part of a community eager to prove its loyalty to the United States. A number of temples and shrines were also taken over during this period of hysteria, and prominent Buddhist priests and lay teachers were removed to mainland internment camps. It was not until long after the end of the war that a reaction of pride in being both Americans and ethnic Japanese took place, allowing the *sansei* and *yonsei*—the third- and fourth-generation Japanese in Hawaii—to take a renewed healthy interest in their Japanese cultural heritage.

*   *   *

It has often been said of Buddhism that it takes on the character of the society in which it finds itself. In the long journey from its Indian origins to Southeast Asia, China, and Japan it has appeared in various guises and colorations. Japanese Buddhism has been distinguished in the main by a concern about power and politics, a strong belief in futurism, and a historically high degree of militancy. But it is noteworthy that its offspring in Hawaii has downgraded these characteristics and emphasized qualities of compatibility and assimilation— which were, it should be added, other attributes of Buddhism in Japan, illustrated by its capacity to coexist in that country with the original folk religion of Shinto.

In Hawaii, Buddhism often appears in its most eclectic, and hence often Westernized, aspects. Many sects have accommodated to the Christian forms: services on Sunday instead of at irregular intervals, the use of pews and pulpits, and even the singing of hymns and anthems to the accompaniment of pipe organs and pianos. The activities of the Young Buddhist Association parallel in many ways those of the YMCA and other Christian organizations. Yet beneath these surface adaptations, the substance of Buddhism in Hawaii remains true to itself. It stresses humility and contemplative meditation, and it teaches the transience of all material things and of existence itself, emphasizing that vanity and selfish desire, which create the pain and dissatisfaction in life, can be overcome through the Eightfold Path of right thought, action, and purpose.

The largest Buddhist group in Hawaii, and perhaps the most representative in its electicism, is the Honpa Hongwanji Mission of the Jodo Shinshu (True Pure Land sect) or Shin (True) sect. Faith is the main tenet of the sect, with particular emphasis on belief in Amida Buddha; this faith is sufficient to guarantee the believer entry into the Pure Land (Jodo), the Western Paradise of Amida. Although its services are now conducted in English as well as Japanese, it nevertheless founded the first Japanese-language school in Hawaii in 1894 at Hilo and later extended the network in other islands. Working in a Hawaiian atmosphere of religious activism, the mission has characteristically added good works to the central doctrine of faith, and the Hongwanji congregation sponsors women's auxiliary groups, Sunday schools, and a gamut of youth activities. It is closely allied to the Jodo (Pure Land) sect and its mission in Hawaii, which unites belief in Amida Buddha with the requirement of helping others to attain enlightenment.

Zen Buddhism, although marked in recent years by a faddish adherence to its discipline by the young everywhere, is the third major sect in Hawaii. It appeals to Asians and Westerners alike, and its emphasis on meditation and self-enlightenment (*satori*) attracts many would-be believers in the contemporary world who disdain formality and ritual. Zen is represented in Hawaii mainly by the Soto Zen Mission, which began its work in the islands in 1913.

The architecture of the main temples of the principal sects mirrors the esoteric and eclectic nature of their development. The Soto Zen temple in Honolulu, built in 1952, is modeled on the Bodhgaya stupa of India, with a highly stylized central pagoda, but it is enhanced by typically Japanese gardens of sand, water, and dwarfed trees (*bonsai*). Indian influence can also be found in the Honpa Hongwanji temple, with its central dome and flanking twin stupas.

In contrast, the Japanese preoccupation with preserving their cultural heritage has resulted in the reproduction on Hawaiian soil of some of the most famous religious and historical structures in Japan. Chief among these is the Phoenix Hall (Byodo-in) on windward Oahu, a faithful recreation in concrete of the original eleventh-century wooden structure that stands at Uji, near Kyoto. Equally remarkable are the reconstruction at Kyoto Gardens in the Nuuanu Valley of the fourteenth-century Golden Pavilion (Kinkaku-ji) of Kyoto and the Kofuku-ji five-story pagoda of Nara. The original Kinkaku-ji was a retreat on the outskirts of Kyoto for one of the Ashikaga shoguns, rulers of Japan in the Muromachi period (1336–1568), but was destroyed by fire in 1950. The reconstruction in Honolulu was overseen by the same architect who directed the rebuilding in Kyoto. Finally, at Lahaina on Maui, the Buddhist Cultural Park of the Lahaina Jodo Mission contains a temple compound with a main hall, a three-story pagoda, and a reduced-scale reproduction of the Great Buddha (Daibutsu) cast in Kamakura, Japan, in the thirteenth century. Both the Byodo-in and the Lahaina temple compound were completed in 1968 to mark the hundredth anniversary of the arrival of the first Japanese immigrants to Hawaii.

The Japanese also brought with them a second faith: the original indigenous set of beliefs known as Shinto, the Way of the Gods. In its purest form, Shinto is a pantheistic amalgam of nature and ancestor worship, expressing a reverence for the forces of nature and an appreciation of man's continuing harmony with them. The concept of *kami*, the divine spirit inherent in all life—in gods and men, in groves, streams, rocks, and hills, and in the sacred products of the fields like rice and wine—is akin to that of the Polynesian mana.

Because of the importance given by Shinto to the idea of lineage and the linking of man with the gods, it was easy for ambitious modern statesmen to distort Shinto in prewar times into a form of emperor worship by claiming that the Japanese sovereign was a direct descendant of the founding gods and goddesses of Japan and the supreme head of a nation-family. Today, Shinto has once again reverted to what it always was, a set of attitudes more individual than congregational in practice, but deeply communal in underlying feeling. Shinto has interacted with and accepted Buddhism as a universal manifestation of its own specific life-respecting quality, and among Japanese it is common to say that one is born and marries in the Shinto way but dies a Buddhist.

Shinto shrines are normally unpretentious and smaller than Buddhist temples. Distinguished by the sacred gate (*torii*) at their entrance, they often stand seemingly empty and silent, with a solitary suppliant in soundless prayer bracketed only by handclaps that call the attention of the gods to the communication being made to them. The architecture is simple and wooden, the materials are often joined without nails, and

Main temple of the Soto Zen Mission of Hawaii, Honolulu (completed 1952)

Wakami Inari shrine, Honolulu

Replica of the pagoda at Kofuku-ji temple, Nara, Japan, in Honolulu (completed 1968)

Copy of the Daibutsu (Great Buddha), Kamakura, Japan, in the Jodo Mission's Buddhist Cultural Park, Lahaina, Maui.

Right and opposite page: Makiki Christian
Church, Honolulu.

Korean Christian Church, Honolulu.

Overleaf: First Chinese Church of Christ, Honolulu.

Saint Luke's Episcopal Church, Honolulu.

Salvation Army chapel, Honolulu.

First United Methodist Church, Honolulu.

Kalikonani Church, the new Catholic
"Church in the Round," Puako, Hawaii

Hawaiian Madonna, a mural by Juliette May Fraser in Saint Catherine's Catholic Church, Kapaa, Kauai.

The Compassionate Christ, a mural by Jean Charlot in
Saint Catherine's Catholic Church, Kapaa, Kauai.

Temple Emanu-El, Honolulu (completed 1950). (Photo by Jean-Paul Chaine)

the austerely vacant interior, usually graced only with the sacred mir-
ror, one of the Three Treasures, reflects the soul of the seeker of truth
back unto himself. Shinto, much like Buddhism but in its own way, thus
affirms the evanescence of all things and the unity of the human and the
divine.

Although the Chinese were the first of the Orientals to arrive in
Hawaii, they were ultimately discouraged by the constantly tightening
restrictions placed on their entry, and around the turn of the century,
when Japanese immigration reached its peak, their numbers actually
declined. Thus they never became a numerically significant element in
the population—even now they are about 53,000 in all, some 7 percent
of the total—but their overall importance greatly outweighs the statis-
tical contribution. The Chinese in Hawaii boast the highest personal
income of any ethnic group, and many of them have become solid pillars
of the community as businessmen, bankers, scholars, and professional
men. The respected position that they have attained in Hawaiian life
today through their unflagging endeavors is a far cry from the pariah
status attached to the first "coolie" immigrants more than a century
ago.

The Chinese, too, brought their religions with them: a syncretic
array of folk beliefs in gods, demons, and myriad spirits, upon which
they had superimposed over the centuries the more abstract philoso-
phies of Taoism, Confucianism, and Buddhism. The magical elements
of Taoism reinforced and explained folk superstitions, while the teachings of Confucius provided a canon of ethics and a code for interpersonal
relations, and even a guide for governing the state. Buddhism produced
a clergy and a spirit of meditation quite different from the mysticism of
the Tao and the practical wisdom of Confucianism. All these elements
were blended together by the Chinese and seasoned with the basic
principle of *yin-yang*, the complementary division of all things into
negative and positive, dark and light, passive and active. They were
then finally placed under the umbrella of the all-pervading family and
ancestor systems, and worshiped at the family shrine. It was as if the
Chinese had sought to take out a broad gamut of insurance against the
evils of this and other worlds and to provide a remedy for each religious
need.

Although Buddhism had long been moribund in China—and indeed
it never took hold there as it did in Japan—when the Chinese began to
arrive in Hawaii, the immigrants were faced with the necessity of

declaring their religion, and the amorphous nature of Chinese beliefs did not lend itself to a simple answer. Some eventually described themselves as Buddhists, leading paradoxically to a minor revival of Chinese Buddhism in the islands in recent times. Others adapted to new circumstances, and as they improved their station in life they sent their children to private Christian schools and allowed them to be baptized in one or another denomination. The new religion could do no harm and it might bring much good to the family. Thus we find Chinese boys and girls among the first enrollees at the Anglican schools, Iolani and St. Andrew's Priory, soon after their arrival in the 1860s, among them Sun Yat-sen, the founder of the Chinese Republic in 1912. It was a Chinese novice who accompanied Bishop Willis to Tonga when he left Hawaii after the American annexation, and a Chinese pastor who founded St. John's Church in the Kula highlands of Maui.

Although the Japanese were more inclined to hold fast to their beliefs than the Chinese, there were Christians among them as well. These Japanese Christians were responsible for one of the most original works of architecture in Hawaii: the Makiki Christian Church of Honolulu, an imposing edifice modeled upon the castle of the Tosa clan on the island of Shikoku, and complete with the turrets and battlements of a medieval Japanese fortress.

The Koreans, last of the East Asian immigrants chronologically and least in number—their count was less than seven thousand in 1940—were the most Christianized of all. The Hermit Kingdom had been the object of intensive and successful missionary attention, and much of the immigration to Hawaii was arranged by the Methodists and the Presbyterians. When Japan annexed Korea in 1910 most Koreans abandoned thoughts of returning home and settled permanently in the islands, which became a home in exile for many Korean political leaders, including Syngman Rhee, the first president of the Republic of Korea after it recovered its independence in 1945. Syngman Rhee lived much of his adult life in Hawaii, and in addition to being hailed as the founding father of his country in modern times, he is remembered as the founder of the Korean Christian Church built in Honolulu along Korean architectural lines. After he died in exile, his funeral was held at the church on Liliha Street before his body was flown back to Korea.

What the various Asian immigrant groups brought to Hawaii is in many ways incalculable. More than anything, they brought themselves and their culture: eager, industrious, hopeful, and talented men and women by the thousands who gave new life to an island kingdom whose own stock was dwindling away from disease and despair as the shock of the meeting with the modern world began to take its toll. But the Orientals not only gave new life to Hawaii, they also gave it a new look that can still be glimpsed today in the arts and ceremonies of their communities. The summer nights resound each weekend at one or another of the Japanese temples to the music and dancing of the Bon festival—the joyful Buddhist wake for the dead in which laughter replaces tears. On the third day of March and the fifth day of May, Japanese girls and boys are honored respectively with the exhibition of dolls and the flying of cloth carp streamers in front of the house. And in the autumn, there can be seen the Shinto Thanksgiving, a descendant of the fall rice-harvest festival of Japan, in which the divine spirit (*kami*) of the shrine is carried about in a portable shrine (*o-mikoshi*) by parishioners in traditional dress so that it may bestow its blessings on the neighborhood.

The Chinese, for their part, have contributed firecrackers and bedlam to the Western New Year's Eve, but more seriously, the celebration of the Chinese New Year in late January or early February, at which time all debts are paid, houses are thoroughly cleaned, and family and community celebrations are held to the accompaniment of dragon dances and general merriment. In September the Chinese Moon Festival commemorates the autumn harvest with round mooncakes, and in October the children of all ethnic groups don traditional dress to participate in the Aloha Week parades that reveal how much Hawaii owes to the many peoples who have created and re-created it with their blood, their sweat, and their love. Hawaii today would be a much poorer place without these gifts that the people of Japan, China, and Korea have conferred upon it. And both those who have given and those who have received are the richer for the result. That the greed of a few sugar planters ultimately became the benefaction of the nation encourages the conviction that God indeed works in wondrous ways.

Epilogue:
The Hawaiis of Today

THE ANCIENT HAWAIIANS could have chosen no more fitting name for the island than Oahu: the Gathering Place. For here, and on the neighboring islands to leeward and windward, the faiths of peoples from the farthest corners of the world have come together and now thrive side by side.

The sects whose history has been narrated in the preceding chapters —Congregational, Catholic, Mormon, Anglican, Buddhist, and Shinto —formed the foundations for the manifold houses of God in modern Hawaii and are the main pillars of these edifices today. But others came and made their contribution as well. The Lutherans arrived through the medium of German immigrants who worked for a sugar plantation on Kauai, and soon wanted a church and school for their children. The Lihue German Lutheran Church, in which only German was originally used, was built in 1883–84 and was for many years the only church of that faith in the islands. Shortly thereafter, in 1885, the Seventh-Day Adventists arrived, and 1894 the Salvation Army, which held open-air services on the steps of the old opera house on Palace Square. Christian Scientists were found in Hawaii in 1902, and after World War I revivalist groups like the Jehovah's Witnesses, with their affirmation of life surviving final destruction, made many converts among the population. At the turn of the century Jewish services were held regularly, and the growing number of adherents after World War II led to the construction of the Temple Emanu-El in Honolulu in 1950.

Through it all Central Union Church, whose present incarnation, built in 1924, stands in stately majesty on the greensward at Beretania and Punahou streets in central Honolulu, has reflected the generous eclecticism of island religious life. Originally Congregational, it has become virtually nondenominational and is known today as the "mother of churches" and of other institutions as well, ranging from the Methodists and the Portuguese Evangelical to the Palama Settlement, the YMCA and YWCA, and the contemporary and socially activist Church of the Crossroads just below the University of Hawaii campus in the Manoa Valley.

From the East came—and still come—Filipinos in a steady flow, mostly within the mainstream of Catholicism, but some also forming evangelical groups that meet in simple country churches and often can be seen working and preaching on the street corners of Honolulu. The syncretic "new religions" of Japan have also made their way to Hawaii: Tenrikyo, which somewhat like Christian Science believes that illness is the result of mental error, has a considerable following among the younger generation of local Japanese Americans; and other faith-healing cults, such as Seicho no Ie (House of Growth), came to the islands in the 1930s and after. From India, Vedanta groups and followers of the Maharishi have appeared, and Hare Krishna devotees are often seen chanting and dancing in the bustling heart of Waikiki today. The universalistic and all-encompassing Baha'i faith, seeking to unite all men without the divisions of religion, not unexpectedly found shelter in the hospitable Hawaiian atmosphere. And just as this chronicle ends, the first foreign mission of the Tendai sect of Japanese Buddhism has dedicated its temple in the Nuuanu Valley of Honolulu, with an imposing sculpture of the thousand-armed Kannon, Bodhisattva of Mercy, standing in the tropical garden and seeming to symbolize the many aspects of divine charity found not only in the temple compound but throughout all Hawaii.

But it was not in the end the Baha'i ideal of unity that prevailed in Hawaii. Rather it was the concept of a diversity of peoples and faiths living in harmony. The always softening effect of the Hawaiian atmosphere tempered the sharp edges of doctrines that had come in antagonism but subsisted in tolerant coexistence, just as it had facilitated the mixing of many bloodstreams and the mingling of many tongues. One may hear the service of the Shin sect in Japanese or English on a Sunday morning, with rituals that are both Buddhist and Christian in inspiration. He may hear the familiar hymns of New England sung in Hawaiian at Kawaiahao, the rock of all churches in Hawaii, or listen to the soft voices of Oriental choirboys in black robes and white collars at the Chinese Christian Church of Honolulu. These and many other manifestations of worship are truly Hawaiian, for Hawaii is what its many peoples and their beliefs have made it. Nationalists, here more than anywhere, are in error: the land is not exclusive, and Hawaiians in heart and mind—Hawaiians by adoption and by choice—stand equal with all others.

But what of those of original Hawaiian stock whose tale began this narrative? They shared their lands generously and gave their blood freely in intermarriage so that even in the shadow of the disappearance of the race they have conserved and passed on to others an intangible spirit that will still fill the land with its grace even when no pureblooded Hawaiian any longer survives. And if it is true, as Aldous Huxley declared, that the advance of humanity from primitiveness to civilization, from mere blood to mind, is both man's greatest accomplishment and one achieved only at a high price, then this transmutation of Hawaiian flesh into Hawaiian spirit is an act of epic proportions, which puts everyone who touches these islands in the eternal debt of the Hawaiians who paid the price.

The old gods did indeed die, but in dying they were transfigured by the alchemy of the Hawaiian spirit, and they emerged as new understandings of the divine, whose prismatic reflections of its multifaceted nature express a composite truth. The faiths of Hawaii today, of the Hawaiis of today that are many and yet at the same time one, incarnate this spirit—which is the true spirit and meaning of *aloha*—and preserve it in diverse ways in their many mansions.

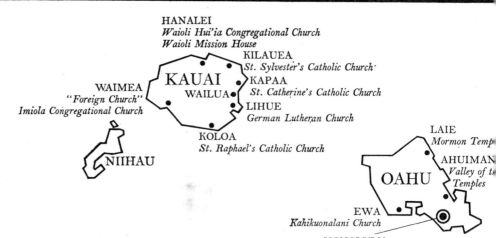

HANALEI
Waioli Hui'ia Congregational Church
Waioli Mission House

KILAUEA
St. Sylvester's Catholic Church·

KAPAA
St. Catherine's Catholic Church

KAUAI

WAIMEA
"Foreign Church"
Imiola Congregational Church

WAILUA

LIHUE
German Lutheran Church

KOLOA
St. Raphael's Catholic Church

NIIHAU

LAIE
Mormon Temp

AHUIMAN
Valley of t
Temples

OAHU

EWA
Kahikuonalani Church

HONOLULU
Cathedral of Our Lady of Peace
Central Union Church
First Chinese Church of Christ
First United Methodist Church
Honpa Hwonganji Mission and Temple
Kaumakapili Church
Kawaiahao Church
Korean Christian Church
Kyoto Gardens
Makiki Christian Church
Mission Houses
Punchbowl Holy Ghost Church
Royal Mausoleum
Salvation Army Chapel
Soto Zen Mission and Temple
St. Andrew's Cathedral
St. Luke's Episcopal Church
Temple Emanu-El
Tendai Mission and Temple
Wakami Inari Shrine

THE HAWAIIAN ISLANDS

PACIFIC OCEAN

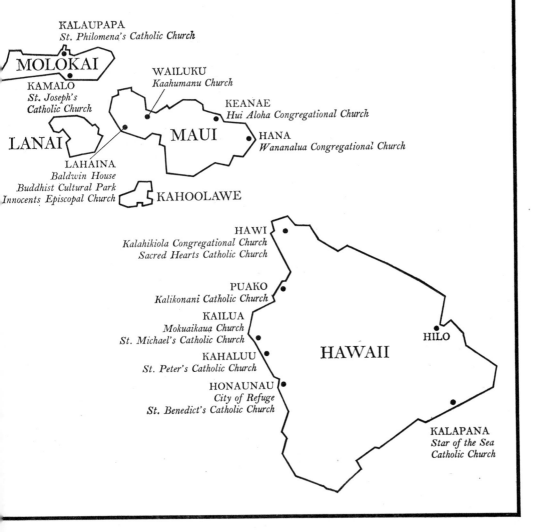

KALAUPAPA
St. Philomena's Catholic Church

MOLOKAI

KAMALO
*St. Joseph's
Catholic Church*

WAILUKU
Kaahumanu Church

KEANAE
Hui Aloha Congregational Church

LANAI

MAUI

HANA
Wananalua Congregational Church

LAHAINA
*Baldwin House
Buddhist Cultural Park
Innocents Episcopal Church*

KAHOOLAWE

HAWI
*Kalahikiola Congregational Church
Sacred Hearts Catholic Church*

PUAKO
Kalikonani Catholic Church

KAILUA
*Mokuaikaua Church
St. Michael's Catholic Church*

KAHALUU
St. Peter's Catholic Church

HONAUNAU
*City of Refuge
St. Benedict's Catholic Church*

HAWAII

HILO

KALAPANA
*Star of the Sea
Catholic Church*

IMPORTANT EVENTS IN HAWAIIAN HISTORY

Voyagers from the Marquesas settle in Hawaii	c. A.D. 750
Colonists from the Society Islands settle in Hawaii	c. 1200
Captain James Cook's expedition discovers Hawaii	January 18, 1778
Kamehameha the Great establishes his rule over all Hawaii	c. 1795
Death of Kamehameha the Great	May 8, 1819
Accession of Kamehameha II (Liholiho)	May 20, 1819

Kamehameha II abolishes the ancient religion and *kapu*	November 1819
First Company of American Congregationalist missionaries arrives	March 31, 1820
Kamehameha II and Queen Kamamalu die in London	July 1824
Accession of Kamehameha III (Kauikeaouli)	June 6, 1825
First Catholic missionaries arrive	July 7, 1827
Declaration of Rights	June 7, 1839
First constitution	October 8, 1840
First Mormon missionaries arrive	December 12, 1850
First Chinese contract laborers arrive	January 3, 1852
Death of Kamehameha III	December 15, 1854
Accession of Kamehameha IV (Alexander Liholiho)	January 11, 1855
First Anglican missionaries arrive	October 11, 1862
Death of Kamehameha IV	November 30, 1863
Accession of Kamehameha V (Lot Kamehameha)	November 30, 1863
First Japanese contract laborers arrive	June 21, 1868
Death of Kamehameha V; end of the Kamehameha dynasty	December 11, 1872

Prince Lunalilo (William Kanaina) is elected king	January 8, 1873
Death of King Lunalilo	February 3, 1874
High Chief David Kalakaua is elected king	February 12, 1874
Reciprocity Treaty with the United States	September 9, 1876
First Portuguese contract laborers arrive	September 13, 1878
First Norwegian and German contract laborers arrive	1881
Soan Kagai, first Japanese Buddhist missionary, arrives	March 2, 1889
First Japanese Buddhist temple is built in Hilo	April 1889
King Kalakaua dies in San Francisco	January 20, 1891
Accession of Queen Liliuokalani	January 29, 1891
Queen Liliuokalani is deposed by provisional government; end of the monarchy	January 17, 1893
Jodo sect of Buddhism is established	1894
Republic of Hawaii is proclaimed	July 4, 1894
Queen Lilioukalani abdicates	January 24, 1895
First Jodo temple is built at Paahau, Hawaii	1896
Honpa Hongwanji of Kyoto establishes Shin sect of Buddhism	October 1897

United States annexes the Hawaiian Islands   July 7, 1898

First Shinto shrine in Hawaii is built in Hilo   1898

First Spanish contract laborers arrive   October 6, 1898

Honpa Hongwanji temple is built in Honolulu   December 1899

Territory of Hawaii is organized   June 14, 1900

Nichiren sect of Buddhism is established   1903

Soto sect of Buddhism is established   1903

First Korean and Filipino contract laborers
arrive   1904–5

Shingon sect of Buddhism is established   1914

Japanese attack on Pearl Harbor begins the
Pacific War   December 7, 1941

Hawaii becomes the fiftieth state   August 21, 1959

The "weathermark" identifies this book
as a production of John Weatherhill, Inc.,
publishers of fine books on Asia and the Pacific.
Supervising editor: Suzanne Trumbull
Book design, typography, and layout of illustrations: Dana Levy
Production supervisor: Mitsuo Okado
Composition and printing: General Printing Company, Yokohama
Offset platemaking and printing: Nissha Printing Company, Kyoto
Binding: Makoto Binderies, Tokyo
The typeface used is Monotype Bell, with Bell for display.